Wholeheartedness

Wholeheartedness

Busyness, Exhaustion, and
Healing the Divided Self

CHUCK DEGROAT

William B. Eerdmans Publishing Company
Grand Rapids, Michigan / Cambridge, U.K.

Published 2016 by

Wm. B. Eerdmans Publishing Co.

2140 Oak Industrial Drive N.E., Grand Rapids, Michigan 49505 /
P.O. Box 163, Cambridge CB3 9PU U.K.

Printed in the United States of America

Library of Congress Cataloging-in-Publication Data

DeGroat, Chuck.

Wholeheartedness: busyness, exhaustion, and healing the divided self /
Chuck DeGroat.

pages   cm

Includes bibliographical references.

ISBN 978-0-8028-7270-8 (pbk.: alk. paper)

1. Self — Religious aspects — Christianity.
2. Christian life.   I. Title.

BT713.D44   2016

248.4 — dc23

2015034804

www.eerdmans.com

Contents

Acknowledgments

When you write a book on wholeheartedness, you cannot possibly do it alone or in a vacuum. Wholeheartedness requires a community, and I've been surrounded by men and women who have shaped me over the past twenty years of ministry and teaching.

That community extends back into the past. You cannot write on wholeheartedness without drinking deeply from St. Augustine, St. Teresa, Rumi, St. John of the Cross, Lady Julian of Norwich, St. Francis, George MacDonald, Søren Kierkegaard, Etty Hillesum, Henri Nouwen, Elizabeth O'Connor, and Thomas Merton. These were conversation partners on my journey. I have also been profoundly influenced by a host of contemporary writers as well (too many to name) — poets, psychologists, neurobiologists, theologians, and more. If there is any wisdom in this work, it is borrowed from others with the hope that I too can be a participant in the wholehearted life I write about here.

But wholeheartedness requires a living and present community too. To know and be known is critical. And so, the honest and courageous voices of good friends like Kyle Small, Brian Keepers, and Jon Brown, though not heard directly in this book, resonate throughout the pages. In the particular season while I was writing this book, these three friends chose to voice wise and hard things to me about my own fragmentation, and as I look back now, I recognize this as a critical moment where two roads diverged in the wood, and where I had to choose wholeheartedness or continuing dis-integration.

I also want to acknowledge the ongoing encouragement of friends and colleagues at the institutions that I serve: Western Theological Seminary and Newbigin House of Studies (as a "Senior Fellow" for City Church San Francisco's city-center ministry partnership with Western Theological Seminary). I can't imagine a wiser or more inspiring array of colleagues.

One's lack of wholeheartedness is exposed, most of all, at home. There, Sara, my extraordinary wife of twenty-one years, and my two daughters, Emma (age 14) and Maggie (age 13), see "all of me." Without their graciousness, love, and patience with me, I couldn't offer a book like this. When they see my contradictions, they don't run away; they continue to love me and allow me to love them. Sara, thank you for believing in me and for your amazingly gentle way with my heart. Emma and Maggie, thank you for the utter delight of being your dad.

Finally, Eerdmans has been a wonderful partner for this book and my previous one. Mary Hietbrink is an editor who brings a relational energy to her work. She encourages, she questions, and she sees what I can't see. I'm grateful to her and to all the folks at Eerdmans for supporting my work.

Permissions

The author and publisher gratefully acknowledge permission to reprint the following:

"Weathering" by Fleur Adcock from *Poems 1960-2000,* published by Bloodaxe Books in 2000. Reproduced with permission of Bloodaxe Books on behalf of the author.

"The Journey" from *Dream Work* by Mary Oliver. Copyright © 1986 by Mary Oliver. Used by permission of Grove/Atlantic, Inc.

"Wild Geese" from *Dream Work* by Mary Oliver. Copyright © 1986 by Mary Oliver. Used by permission of Grove/Atlantic, Inc.

"Love after Love" from *The Poetry of Derek Walcott, 1948-2013* by Derek Walcott, selected by Glyn Maxwell. Copyright © 2014 by Derek Walcott.

Introduction

I'm being pulled in a thousand different directions.

I hear this all the time.

I hear it from students and software developers. I hear it from stay-at-home mothers and fathers. I hear it from the underemployed, the unemployed, and the overemployed. I hear it from those who make seven figures, and those who covet that life. I hear it from spiritual leaders and coffee baristas. And, not surprisingly, I hear it from the therapists, pastors, and rabbis who counsel all of these frazzled folks.

We all feel that nasty pull, that pull to and fro, as if we'll come undone at some point.

When it comes to the important resource of time, we feel dirt poor. Most of you reading this book are quite affluent and well-resourced relative to the rest of the global world, where taking the time to read a book like this would be an unthinkable luxury. But *time* is a different kind of resource. We feel the scarcity of this precious good, one which doesn't discriminate on the basis of ethnicity or religion or economic status.

Perhaps we feel a bit like Dr. Seuss, who writes,

How did it get so late so soon?
It's night before it's afternoon.
December is here before it's June.
My goodness how the time has flewn.
How did it get so late so soon?[1]

No matter who we are or how ingenious or successful we may be, we can't work hard enough to earn more time. We can't buy more time. And we can't control time, which might be the hardest reality of all to accept. For control is what we long for, evidenced in the plethora of time-saving and time-managing programs and gadgets constantly produced, each more ridiculous than the last one. Recently I became convinced that an iWatch would at last be the "miracle cure" for my compulsion to control. Soon enough, I may fall into that trap too.

As we will see, we often experience our lives as *divided*. Feeling pulled in a thousand different directions, we wonder if a sense of balance and harmony is possible. We long for an elusive wholeness. And I believe that wholeness is more essential to who we are than our neuron-firing brains and our beating hearts. So in this book we'll explore these inner divisions and pave a pathway to wholeness and flourishing.

Seeking an Elusive Wholeness

These days there's a market for wholeness. Google the word and you'll find books and videos, ministries and institutes, educational programs and scientific theories. The interest in wholeness has become so pervasive that, during the fifteen years I've been doing clinical counseling, I've noticed a definite shift in the way my clients speak. They often talk about becoming more *whole* or *wholehearted* or experiencing greater *wholeness*. And sometimes I'm suspicious. Many of our cultural ideas about wholeness are conjured by some crazy and creepy dealers in the life-of-flourishing market.

But despite the bad ideas floating around out there, I'm noticing much that is positive in what I'm hearing. Much of what I share in this book is what I've learned about the divided life and the elusive wholeness people long for, and I hope it can be helpful to you.

Over the past fifteen years, I've tried to listen — to listen well and listen with genuine curiosity — to hundreds, maybe thousands of people who I can call friends and clinical clients and parishioners and mentees and students. And I've tuned into my own heart in a very deep way while researching and writing this book during the last year — which has been illuminating, because I've often been flying here and there and everywhere to speak, so sometimes I've been exhausted and divided myself. As I told a friend recently, I've been my own research subject. I've often found myself, bleary-eyed, on a United Airlines flight, either quietly contemplating my own inner state from a place of solitude and compassion, or fiercely highlighting pages and pages of books and articles — frantically trying to excel at one more thing but just exhausting myself in the process.

There are three very important things that I want to share with you at the outset. I want to show my cards, so to speak, so that you'll know what you're in for.

First, there is an extraordinary underlying unity to what I'm seeing on this subject. Let me explain. It seems that whoever the perspective comes from — a sociologist or a neurobiologist or a physicist or a theologian or a psychologist — there are similar themes and patterns which make me think that those who are musing on wholeness are reading each other's mail. And while there's always someone adding toxins to the melting pot of ideas, there's surprising unity among scholars across disciplines on the division and fragmentation we experience, and the wholeness we long for.

As a person of faith, I'm not surprised by this. In fact, in my research for this book, I found researchers and philosophers and poets stumbling into the same reality, a reality that's begging us to see the inherent wholeness amid fragmentation and division. In fact, as I was completing this book, a friend prompted me to read at least part of a book that I discovered was one of the great late-twentieth-century works on science and philosophy: *Wholeness and the Implicate Order* by David Bohm.

Bohm, a theoretical physicist, found that wholeness undergirds the deep divisions which show up on a psychic and social level; he proposes that, by and large, our fragmentation is manufactured based on function and practicality. He calls attention to the Hebrew worldview and the foundational idea of *shalom,* citing it as a signpost of wholeness embedded in an ancient tradition. In noting how this fundamental wholeness has been sabotaged by division, Bohm writes, "Surely, the question of why all this has come about requires careful attention and serious consideration."[2] I hope that Bohm would consider this book among those giving this idea serious attention, while at the same time offering fresh perspectives and practices for those wrestling with the symptoms of a divided life — exhaustion, loneliness, even despair.

So, beyond the cross-disciplinary agreement I'm seeing, I've been struck by a second theme. It caught me by surprise, but it's one that encourages me greatly. What researchers are finding, as we will see, is that there is a very definite movement from an emphasis on self-esteem to an emphasis on self-compassion. And as a person of faith, I find this to be a movement toward a more substantial understanding of the human person.

A leading and influential researcher and popularizer of this idea is Dr. Brené Brown, a research professor at the University of Houston's Graduate College of Social Work. What Brown and other social researchers are telling us is that we've worked so hard to gain approval and esteem that we're now crushed under the heavy burdens of fear, shame, and a lack of self-worth. What Brown and others are finding is that we've traded our longing to belong for the quick fix of fitting in. We've traded wholeness for perfectionism.

The need to belong is in our DNA, a primitive instinct that roots us in community, identity, and purpose. But in trading belonging for the fix of fitting in, we've fractured our very selves, cutting ourselves into pieces for the roles we think we're supposed to play, each with a unique mask we think we're supposed to wear. And this inner division creates a fertile soil in which symptoms like exhaustion, burnout, perfectionism, purposelessness, anxiety, and depression can grow.[3] Brown's research, among others, encourages a new kind of journey in which the goal of growth in self-esteem is replaced by a more generous and compassionate understanding of all that is broken and messy and unlovable within us.

And here's the third thing: I'm struck by what I see in my own faith tradition — Christianity. Now, stick with me here. If you're reading from the perspective of another faith tradition, you might assume I'll be going against the popular grain in what follows. But here's what I've found: Wholeness is essential to the Christian tradition. Admittedly, we who call ourselves "Christian" are fairly poor examples of wholeness. I suppose we offer examples of shaming and blaming far more than we offer examples of flourishing. But I'm not going to apologize for that. What I will do is agree that we've got to take our medicine. We're a messy bunch who proclaim grace but pursue perfectionism, who long for wholeness but seek to achieve it through a distorted form of holiness. We need *your* grace as well as God's grace, because we've failed to offer you the better hope of a God who is whole and holy, and whose greatest task is to make us whole and holy.

And so I'll explore themes from my own tradition. And I'll even address why now, perhaps more than ever, it's critical for Christians to stop perpetuating the tradition of division we've become known for. This won't be easy: it will require Christians to re-engage their tradition, re-commit to a hearty and whole engagement with their churches, and re-imagine holiness not through the lens of perfectionism but through the lens of our utter oneness with God.

Falling into Wholeness

My own journey toward wholeness feels less like a goal I'm attaining and more like a continual falling and failing which, paradoxically, leads to surrender and self-compassion. Now in my midforties, I thought I'd have things much more together than I do today. I completed a Master of Divinity degree in the mid-1990s, but I quickly discovered that I had not, in fact, *mastered* the divine. I was an arrogant, self-righteous, very anxious young man who might get a job preaching grace, but who had no business taking it, because I'd be a prophet of perfectionistic holiness.

Thankfully, I stumbled into a space where wholeness might grow. A series of relational disappointments led me into the office of a counseling professor named Gary. He told me what I was terrified to hear: I wasn't ready. I wasn't ready for pastoral life, I wasn't ready for real relationships — I wasn't even ready for the marriage I'd been in for over three years. In fact, he told me I'd probably hurt myself, my marriage, and the church if I went into ministry.

And so I did what every sane and healthy person does — I entered therapy, repented of my many sins and failures, and turned to a life of wholeness!

No. No, I didn't. Instead, I applied for Gary's clinical counseling graduate program. I thought that this advanced training might give me some time to work through my issues discreetly and also help me get another degree. My inner perfectionist was too committed to saving face, to maintaining my reputation as someone who had it all together.

So I entered this clinical counseling program, playing the new part I thought I should play, but hoping, desperately hoping, that I'd get fixed. I stumbled through it. I didn't know the steps like I did in my theological degree program, where if you mastered the material you were accepted. Instead, I was exposed time and again for wearing the many masks I'd created in my first twenty-seven years of life. Gary and others were inviting me to know and be known — to God, to my wife, to my clinical colleagues who were also navigating this tangled way of transformation.

But being known is a terribly uncomfortable thing. So I invented new masks — the mask of the competent therapist, the wise sage, and the emotionally attuned soul. And I kept falling. Usually I'd notice the signs too late. I'd notice after my reactive outburst, after my season of burnout, after my many weeks of disconnection both internally and externally. I began to see that wholeness wasn't just another project to be completed, but more like a soft place to land when I'd fallen again, shattering my latest mask. As a man who had apparently mastered divinity in three years, I was discovering that wholeness came as I fell into God, into a kind of union and belonging and intimacy I'd never known before.

This journey still scares me. But it's also slowly and steadily opening me to something new, a longed-for wholeness I found so elusive.

Here's what I'm learning personally about wholeness. I'm learning that it can't be managed. It can't be scheduled. It can't be attained in seven easy steps or three key disciplines. And while disciplines and boundaries and wise life choices are building blocks of a life well-lived, we learn wholeness, more often than not, when our boundaries are shattered, when our disciplines fail us, when our theologies stump us, when our supposedly wise choices betray us. We learn by un-learning, by stumbling and falling into the very thing we attempted to gain on our own terms. This, I believe, is the deep wisdom of my Christian tradition.

Like love, wholeness is discovered in a thousand disappointments, embarrassments, and missteps. It's discovered as our egos are shattered in the inviting presence of Another, One who calls us to belong. It's experienced as a unity within ourselves and with our world that is indescribably satisfying.

While I sought to master divinity, Divinity sought to love me. But it takes a lifetime to be broken of our ego-and-control addictions, which do in fact lead to the madness of a divided life.

Understanding Wholeheartedness

As I grew into wholeness through clinical training and ongoing therapy, I found it increasingly difficult to exist within structures that perpetuated shame. Even in places where words like "Gospel" and "grace" were named, a culture of shame continued to exist. For a time I wondered if I even belonged anymore. I had become a pastor, but I pastored ambivalently and cautiously. This disconnect led to a larger vocational ambivalence, which in turn made me more and more anxious and fatigued. I needed help. Again.

A colleague told me that I'd benefit from the work of the poet David Whyte — in particular, his *Poetry of Self-Compassion*.[4] I'll never forget listening to a CD of Whyte's musings for the first time and hearing him tell a very important story, a story that marked a turning point in his own exhausting work for a nonprofit. That became a defining moment for me, too.

Over a glass of wine, Whyte said to his friend, Brother David Steindl-Rast, "Tell me about exhaustion."

Steindl-Rast, a monk and spiritual director, responded, "You know that the antidote to exhaustion is not necessarily rest?"

Whyte froze in his tracks — and I did, too. My first thought was, *Really? No, rest is the antidote. . . . We all know that — the Bible says so. That settles it.*

Fatigued and somewhat puzzled, Whyte mustered up the energy to respond: "The antidote to exhaustion is not necessarily rest? What is it, then?" I sat anxiously on the edge of my chair, waiting for the monk's sage advice.

Brother Rast responded, "The antidote to exhaustion is wholeheartedness."[5]

Wholeheartedness.

And then I saw everything clearly. I saw myself working tirelessly and perfectionistically, exhausting myself as I tried to tell people that Jesus offers *grace* and *rest*. And my own hypocrisy was exposed. I was living the divided life. I was the phony, the "hypocrite," as Jesus calls the religious leaders, the actor wearing masks in his public life while fiercely guarding his private life, his heart. I wasn't wholehearted. And that prevented me from finding any real and deep rest.

True rest was something I didn't know how to do. I could stop my usual activities. I could watch a football game on a Sunday afternoon. I could even take a nap. But these things could not and would not stop the frenzied inner activity that continued incessantly. In my divided soul, true "rest" didn't have a fighting chance.

I've spent more than a decade listening, praying, researching, practicing, and failing at wholeness. And the result is this book.

In the coming chapters, I'll let you in on some of what I've learned about dividedness and wholeness, exhaustion and rest, shame and perfectionism. In the first part, we'll look at what sociologists, psychologists, neurobiologists, and researchers of many different stripes are saying about these very things. There's a very important and exciting conversation taking place that you need to know about. It offers insights into how we experience exhaustion and dividedness, and how we're literally hard-wired to thrive in wholeness.

In the second part, we'll shift gears, turning our attention first to what poets and sages have said about the divided life. And then we'll see how this wisdom is shared by Jesus, who overturned tables and broke long-held boundaries in order to bring wholeness to the most broken. We'll tie this conversation to the first one by considering a new kind of *Christian psychology* of wholeness.[6] If you're reading this and you don't share my faith tradition, I'm not here to proselytize. I just want to re-narrate my own tradition in a way that I think you might find intriguing.

In the third part, we'll look at the practices that cultivate wholeness. What I'll share with you is what I've learned from a variety of sources, but most importantly from three primary sources: the contemplative tradition; a fairly new and remarkably helpful psychological system called Internal Family Systems Theory; and the Christian liturgical tradition. These three may seem like strange bedfellows, but, as I've said, there's an astounding convergence we can discover among them.

I've been watching this convergence, but I've also had plenty of practice in the trenches with those who've allowed me to pastor them, to counsel them, to teach and to dialogue with them. And this journey wouldn't be possible without diagnosing our unwholeness.

Part 1

DIAGNOSING OUR *UN*WHOLENESS

feeling pulled in a thousand different directions

. . . this is how it feels to live my life: scattered, fragmented, and exhausting. I am always doing more than one thing at a time and feel I never do any one particularly well.

BRIGID SCHULTE

Shame works like the zoom lens on a camera. When we are feeling shame, the camera is zoomed in tight, and all we see is our flawed selves, alone and struggling.

BRENÉ BROWN

Every night you're trying to prove your self-worth. It's like meeting your girlfriend's family for the first time. You want to be the absolute best, wittiest, smartest, most charming, best-smelling version of yourself. If I can make people enjoy the experience and have a higher regard for me when I'm finished, it makes me feel like an entire person. If I've come short of that, I'm not happy. How things go for me every night is how I feel about myself for the next 24 hours.

DAVID LETTERMAN

BENEATH THE FRENZIED ACTIVITY and the frantic thoughts that dominate our daily lives exists a quiet voice. Frightened, we ignore it, particularly when it's a mere whisper. Our tasks and to-do lists keep us dulled to its pulsing, inner existence.

In a moment of pause, we may hear it. In the quiet of an elevator ride up to our office. In the few minutes it takes for our morning coffee to brew. In the darkness as we drift off to sleep. In a hot shower as we get ready for work.

I'm not doing enough.
I should appreciate my family more.
I'm not impressive enough at the office.
I don't know what I should know at this point in my life.

In these moments, the quiet voice roars into our consciousness like an unwanted stranger. It feels like an enemy. Sometimes we tell it to go away. Sometimes we *will* it to go away. Sometimes our next activity dulls it once again. But it doesn't leave. It won't leave. It's our heart's constant companion — shame — awakening us to what we'd rather avoid or deny about ourselves. But we're adept at hitting the snooze button.

Reminded by this voice that we're not doing enough or impressive enough or knowledgeable enough, we double down. We organize our desks. We comb through our calendars and e-mails looking for something we've missed. We check in with others for approval. We look for Retweets on Twitter. We rethink our strategy. Or we make a deal with God: *I'll give you my best if you give me yours.*

Doubling down, we temporarily squelch the annoying whispers. With a few small successes, we feel a surge of dopamine glory that fuels our addictive patterns of busyness, a sense that we've conquered the supposed enemy within. We ride this new wave as long as we can. Maybe it lasts hours, maybe even days. But sooner or later, the annoying ache is triggered again, perhaps by a deadline reminder or a critical e-mail or a silence that lasts a bit too long.

This time, it's the inner voice that doubles down. Instead of saying *I'm not doing enough,* the stranger within offers a more troubling observation.

I'm not enough.

This isn't an accusation that arises just in our minds. No, we feel it in our bodies: it burns in our chests. It's palpable. And the accusation is born of shame, perhaps the most violating inner stranger of them all. We hate this unwanted stranger because it makes us hate ourselves. And we want more than anything to get rid of it. We would if we could. And some of us try, through cutting, or binging and purging, or even performing a religious ritual.

In these moments, we feel as if we're the only people on earth who feel such self-disgust, such self-loathing. There may be no other emotional response more isolating, more lonely than this one. And it can happen amid success, applause, and high regard.

The longtime late-night TV host David Letterman once reflected on his own inner battle:

> Every night you're trying to prove your self-worth. It's like meeting your girlfriend's family for the first time. You want to be the absolute best, wittiest, smartest, most charming, best-smelling version of yourself. If I can make people enjoy the experience and have a higher regard for me when I'm finished, it makes me feel like an entire person. If I've come short of that, I'm not happy. How things go for me every night is how I feel about myself for the next 24 hours.[1]

We all know this inner stranger, this seemingly incurable virus called shame. It makes us feel completely revealed as the flawed selves we are, utterly exposed in our idiosyncrasies and inadequacies.

In her breakthrough book *The Gifts of Imperfection,* Brené Brown writes, "Shame works like the zoom lens on a camera. When we are feeling shame, the camera is zoomed in tight, and all we see is our flawed selves, alone and struggling."[2] Shame feels like a kind of slime that clings tenaciously to us, impossible to wash away.

I believe that its presence is the fuel for our perfectionism, which ultimately leads us to burnout and exhaustion. In shame, we hide behind masks that protect us from ourselves and others. In shame, we live divided lives that rob us of wholeness and peace. Divided and fragmented, we work tirelessly to perfect ourselves but only end up exhausting ourselves. This is our common story. No one is immune.

A Desperate Hunger

Henry David Thoreau famously said, "The mass of men lead lives of quiet desperation." But what he said next is most telling:

> What is called resignation is confirmed desperation. From the desperate city you go into the desperate country, and have to console yourself with the bravery of minks and muskrats. A stereotyped but unconscious despair is concealed even under what are called the games and amusements of mankind. There is no play in them, for this comes after work. . . .[3]

Desperation and shame go hand in hand. We may not look desperate to our co-worker, our stock advisor, or our spouse, but we feel desperate. We are desperate to keep shame tamped down and desperate when it flares up again.

Think about it this way. Because we believe shame to be the enemy, we fight it. We conceal our shame in our addictions, our work, our amusements, our social-media selves, our cosmetic improvements. We pursue numerous social activities, perhaps afraid of what solitude might reveal within. We hide behind a forced smile. But somewhere beneath all this busyness and show, we know the truth. *We're barely keeping it together.* Rather than admit our desperate state, however, we end our days with a few too many glasses of wine and a double shot of Advil PM, hoping we'll be fuzzy enough to forget as we drift into sleep.

Washington Post journalist Brigid Schulte conducted a comprehensive social study on the phenomenon of our frantic and fragmented lives. In her study she spent time with a well-regarded leader in work and leisure research who "likens modern American culture to the aimless whirl of ants whose anthill has just been stomped on." The brainless rushing about makes us feel time-starved, which "does not result in death, but rather, as ancient Athenian philosophers observed, in never beginning to live."[4]

Do you sometimes feel like an aimless ant? Do you sometimes wonder if you're really *living* or merely *surviving*?

When I was living and working in San Francisco, I started a counseling center. Many of the men and women to whom I was privileged to offer care had wealth and privilege unlike anything I'll ever know. But what was common among all the people I counseled, no matter what their level of economic and social class, was a sense that something was missing. Many of them were entrepreneurs who put in sixty to eighty hours a week or more at the office, then continued their work from home at night, never disconnecting from the technological matrix which provided income, identity, and belonging. Because their spiritual and emotional welfare was an afterthought, it took a crisis to reveal the dark underbelly of desperation, meaninglessness, and emptiness they really felt. What I would see on social media were sparkling personas, but behind closed doors I experienced their shame — the shame of unmet expectations, difficult relationships, bruised egos, and deep dissatisfaction.[5] Success wasn't enough to soothe the deep ache, the great hunger within.

But it's profoundly counter-intuitive to admit the desperation, to listen to the unwanted stranger within. We'll invariably flee from desperation rather than admit our need. Or we'll turn our deep need into a shallow want and find a quick fix to satiate it. Like a ravenous teenager, we'll satisfy the immediate hunger pangs with a drive-through cheeseburger thirty minutes before dinner rather than waiting for the feast that Dad and Mom are preparing at home.

Desperation leads to a sense of scarcity. Instead of courageously leaning in to our heart's deepest fear — *I'm not enough* — we project outward, into people or things that might satisfy the ache, the hunger, even for a brief moment. Indeed, what researchers find is that scarcity is a common experience among the seemingly happiest and wealthiest among us.[6] Scarcity — a word once reserved to describe the plight of the most impoverished — is now a word that describes First-World consumers like us. No, we're not clamoring for basic things like food, water, and shelter. What we claim we need and what we claim we lack are two different things.

I hear it every time a person I'm meeting with pushes aside the opportunity to feast on his or her deeper life in favor of the fast-food cheeseburger of a short-term solution or an immediate fix. Think about how many times you'll say things like this to yourself:

I just need an iPhone to stay in better touch with my family.
I just need a vacation to recharge my batteries.
I just need that raise to get to a place where I'll feel secure.
I just need to lose ten pounds to feel better about myself.

Running from the opportunity to draw from the deep well of our mysterious inner lives pulsing with both shame and glory, we treat that rising ache from within as something to quiet as quickly as we can. And our instinct is reinforced by legions of quick-fix burger peddlers whispering, like the ancient serpent, "Don't wait for the feast. You know you want *this.*"

We now know that each year millions of dollars are spent on psychological research to determine what you and I hunger for, and that marketers use this research to custom-tailor ads that will stir longing in us.[7] The General Motors' research division once called this "the organized creation of dissatisfaction."[8] On streaming Internet services, we're even asked "Do you like this ad?" — a phenomenon that allows advertisers to determine which ads are most effective. This very intentional manipulation of human desire hides quietly behind a billions-of-dollars-a-year marketing industry, geared to creating dissatisfaction and perceived needs in you and me.

The industry targets our sense of shame.

> You need to look better, produce more, win more, buy more, and improve your sex life.
> You're not enough without a hotter body, a better car, a closer shave, and fresher breath.

Because we're fueled by the belief that we're not enough, parts of us go into overdrive, frantically seeking the satisfaction we crave in more success, a better body, or the approval of others. But like the fast-food customer, in the end we're left lethargic, tired, and hungry for something more.

Indeed, I believe that we're created with deep desires that express themselves in our many longings, whether for beauty, success, security, or love.[9] We long desperately for happiness, for satisfaction, for meaning. Our desperation would be easy to diagnose and "fix" if it were merely a problem of "wanting too much." But because we refuse to honor the ache within and all the questions it raises, we settle for too little.

And we're left with the stark reality that many of us aren't really living, that many of us remain desperately hungry for more, and that, despite our shiny smiles, many of us aren't *really* happy.

Shiny, Happy People

The other day I asked my daughters, who are fourteen and thirteen, what the happiest place in the world was. I'm thankful that they didn't say "Disney World." But the three of us did start talking about family vacations and about the places we've lived: Orlando, San Francisco, and that idyllic city-by-the-lake called Holland, Michigan. Then I asked, "What's the happiest country on earth?" Both of them looked a bit puzzled. Then one said, "The United States, of course." After all, in the scarcity model, we're the country that has it all — according to the media, our leaders, and our preachers. We judge every other nation as having less.

I took the question a bit further. "Let's play a game," I suggested. "You tell me which country is happier. We'll start with an easy one: the United States or Rwanda?"

This was easy but sad: my girls knew about the genocide and political strife in Rwanda. Most of our kids (I hope) are aware at some level of First-World and Third-World differences. After this softball, I threw them a curveball.

"Canada or the United States?"

"Hmmm. Probably the United States. Canada has a lot, but not as much as we have."

(Please note: Their answers are telling. The advertisers are already getting to them!)

"Actually, Canada is happier than we are," I said. "Mexico or the United States?"

"Probably the United States," they said again. They recalled a time when we were in Mexico and I needed emergency surgery. We were all a bit worried about the level of medical care I'd receive, and were quickly forced to deal with our "better than" assumption about technological superiority, an assumption that sooner or later leads to moral superiority. But in some significant ways, Mexico is superior. "Mexico is happier than the United States," I told them.

Then I showed them a United Nations study detailing the rankings.[10] My daughters were shocked that the United States ranked below Mexico, Canada, and even Israel, despite the political and social unrest there. And the five happiest countries on earth? Denmark, Norway, Switzerland, the Netherlands, and Sweden. The United States didn't make the top five. They were shocked again. The categories they'd developed for happiness and unhappiness were suddenly challenged.

These questions and answers got us talking about happiness — how we experience it, what it means, what we long for. I explained to them that the U.N. study had based its rankings of happiness on six key factors: real GDP per capita, healthy life expectancy, having someone to count on, perceived freedom to make life choices, freedom from corruption, and generosity. We talked about happiness as more than "having things" and explored its connection to the key factors in the study. I thought back to what Brené Brown had said — that perhaps we're all striving to fit in rather than to belong. Could it be that in the places ranked most happy, people feel less pressure to be brilliant architects of their perfect-looking lives?

Of course, we don't need U.N. data to tell us that the U.S. isn't the happiest country. We're living data. We see the proof in our grumpiness after an extraordinary Caribbean vacation, in our lack of lasting satisfaction even after a good review from the boss, in our reactive rage to the simplest things going just a bit wrong. We feel it in our buyer's remorse after taking out a mortgage too big for our budget, in the mild irritation we experience when our coworker co-opts the microwave, in our stuffed but unsatisfied stomachs after a McDonald's binge.

Late in life, the Catholic writer and mystic Thomas Merton wrote, "Man in our day, menaced on all sides with ruin, is at the same time beset with illusory promises of happiness."[11] And he's right: our common story includes a struggle to experience that illusive happiness promised in political speeches and television ads and televangelists' sermons. Our common story includes settling for fleeting satisfactions rather than paying attention to the deeper longings which beg for expression.

We exhaust ourselves in the restless pursuit of something that will satisfy. And tragically, we sometimes resist and sabotage real living and real freedom when they're offered to us.

Do We Want to Rest?

Brigid Schulte's research fascinates me. Gathering data from a variety of reputable sources, she puts into words what I hear in counseling sessions and classrooms. Schulte reports that seniors, who ought to be teaching the rest of us how to enjoy life, "felt flattened by all the tasks they needed and wanted to do in a day."[12] And 40 percent of American workers, no matter their socio-economic status, feel overworked. Americans feel they work longer and in more extreme conditions than in any other industrialized country. Half of all workers feel like they have too much work to finish in a typical week. Two-thirds report not having enough time with their spouse, and three-fourths report not having enough time with their children.

But do we want real, satisfying rest? Apparently not. While we crave that desperately needed vacation which promises sun, sand, and fun, research shows that most of us work on vacation. In many cases, it seems, busyness addicts simply don't use their vacation, despite the daily groanings of "I just need to get away!" Schulte notes that a combination of bad policies and bad choices we make puts "the United States simultaneously at the bottom of the global list for vacation time offered and at the top of the list for workers who throw those vacation days away."[13] Consequently, she reports, "An increasing number of workers reported feeling overwhelmed, in poorer health, overworked, depressed, angry at their employers for expecting so much, resentful of others they thought were slacking off, and being so exhausted that they were prone to making mistakes and doing lower-quality work."[14]

Schulte's comprehensive survey took her to both large metropolitan areas and rural towns, but she found the same phenomenon everywhere she went. Scarcity doesn't discriminate among rich and poor, those in big cities and those in small towns. And shame knows no boundaries. Perfectionism exists in both your first-grader and your grandpa. And in today's complex, technologically inundated society, which allows us to be seen, connected, updated, followed, and accessed anywhere and anytime, we certainly don't experience the freedom and rest and spaciousness that we say we want. As Harmut Rosa points out, "The history of modernity seems to be characterized by a wide-ranging speed-up of all kinds of technological, economic, social, and cultural processes and by a picking up of the general pace of life."[15] And with powerful cultural forces at work, it may take more than good intentions for us to make a significant shift in our lives.

Elusive Freedom, Elusive Happiness

In my first book, *Leaving Egypt*,[16] I suggested that we're all quite adept at a kind of mindless self-sabotage. I called it "Stockholm syndrome of the soul," a condition whereby we remain in the kinds of awful, dead-end, difficult relationships and jobs and places that suck the life out of us. Much like the Israelites of old, we go back to Egypt, back to a place of enslavement, back to the place that promises some semblance of security and well-being, even though we're frogs in a slowly boiling pot awaiting our imminent doom.

As it turns out, our common story is more than just a modern American story — it's an ancient one, too. It's a universal story that says something about our human condition and our propensity to sabotage freedom. Philosopher Nicolas Berdyaev writes,

> Humanity is in a state of servitude. We frequently do not notice that we are slaves, and sometimes we love it. But humanity also aspires to be set free. It would be a mistake to think that the average person loves freedom. A still greater mistake would be to suppose that freedom is an easy thing. Freedom is a difficult thing.[17]

The U.N. Happiness Report got me thinking about freedom again, this time in a new way. It seems that our perceived freedom has a direct correlation to our happiness. And as I thought about the different factors in the report — freedom from corruption, freedom to make life choices, generosity, and so on — I began to wonder what really enslaves us at a societal level. I began to wonder, in fact, how we really understand freedom.

Of course, we sometimes see freedom in terms of financial security. This is much sought after as a key to happiness and a well-lived life. I need only proudly pull out my Chase Freedom credit card to remind myself of this, though I don't feel very free when the monthly bill arrives. The Internet is chock full of "financial freedom" schemes, each one offering its proven pathway to the lifestyle that Americans desire. And if you turn on cable news, you'll hear debates about freedom and the so-called free market, a mysterious force with a personality all its own, promising to pay off most when we work the hardest and when we're least burdened by limits and regulations.[18]

Perhaps financial freedom can rescue us from that menacing ache within? Perhaps we think so until we read that astounding U.N. report featuring countries where financial freedom is defined quite differently — where wealth is redistributed, where vacations are mandatory and long, where income equality reduces the panic and shame of competition, and where public policies do seem to be making important lifestyle differences. But surely some perfect economic utopia isn't the key to happiness, is it?

I also thought about how many times we all say, "If only I had more time." We believe that having enough time, like having enough money, is our key to a happy and flourishing life. With every scheme for financial freedom comes the promise of "making more money in less time." We're continually looking for ways to get time back, yet we feel it slipping away. We long for the long weekend, and yet it flies by. We think to ourselves, *Surely Americans today have far less time than they did fifty years ago!* Time becomes the idol promising that elusive freedom from the desperation we feel.

And yet researcher John Robinson has found that Americans are not, in fact, losing time. In *Time for Life: The Surprising Way Americans Use Their Time,* Robinson, through detailed case studies and time diaries, shows that Americans actually have *more* time than they did in the 1960s.[19] How we *use* our time is the critical issue here, and Robinson's study asks very practical questions about what we do and when we do it. Robinson points out that we can learn much about just how much time we're "losing" if we pay attention to our television and social-media habits, among other things. But Robinson's study provides no clear remedy for time-hungry folks like you and me. Perhaps finding more time isn't the ultimate salve?

I thought about money and I thought about time. But I also thought about how we expect political figures to increase our freedoms, and soldiers to fight for our freedoms, and doctors to free us from signs of age, and self-help books to free us from anxiety, and pills to free us from sleeplessness.

What's important to recognize is that we perceive our lives to be happy, fulfilled, and free through a particular story or lens, and we're willing to go to great lengths to find it. We define happiness and freedom in certain fixed ways. This is why the clients I work with often give me a funny look when I throw a grenade into their best-laid plans for satisfaction and ask them to return to a deeper dialogue in their hearts. I know what they're thinking: *Won't that just get in the way?* Perhaps we're far more addicted than we think we are to those "drive-throughs" to satisfaction.

Divided, We Struggle

We cannot long nostalgically for some idyllic past. As we've seen, busyness isn't a new phenomenon, and perfectionism isn't an American invention. Humanity's struggle with labor and toil is primeval, as the story in Genesis 3 shows us. We cannot simply blame advertisers or politicians or economists or the rich for our exhaustion. And, as it turns out, we can't simply say, "There's just no time anymore!"

So, what can we say? What we'll explore, from here on out, is both a core reality of our experience *and* an abiding psychological and spiritual reality named by philosophers, poets, and priests. It helps us understand our perceived lack of freedom. It makes sense of the deep dissatisfaction we experience. It puts shame and perfectionism in context. It affirms what neurobiologists are learning about how human brains organize experience.

Without exploring the many dimensions of it, Brigid Schulte names this culprit at the very beginning of her dense work on human busyness. She writes,

> . . . this is how it feels to live my life: scattered, fragmented, and exhausting. I am always doing more than one thing at a time and feel I never do any one particularly well. I am always behind and always late, with one more thing and one more thing and one more thing to do before rushing out the door. Entire hours evaporate while I'm doing stuff that needs to get done. But once I'm done, I can't tell you what it was I did or why it seemed so important.[20]

Scattered. Fragmented. Exhausting. Schulte names the *divided life*. And this is a reality that everyone I've counseled, pastored, or taught can identify with.

This is the reality of the mother who wears the multiple hats of breadwinner, diaper-changer, board member, chauffeur to her teenage children, counselor to her under-employed husband, and chief chef to the family.

This is the reality of the husband who sits in front of a computer screen with ten different windows open. Each window reflects a different part of his fragmented life. He jumps from a work spreadsheet to the home finances, from uploading personal pictures to Facebook to updating Twitter, from adding new apps for his children to e-mailing his aging parents.

This is the reality that many of us who live far from our birthplaces experience. Separated from family and childhood support systems, we reinvent ourselves in new communities and new places

— at college, at our first job, in the new town we're transferred to, in the city we move to for the dream job — where our identities always seem to be shifting.

This is the reality of the multi-tasking commuter who's on a conference call as he eats his fast-food breakfast while driving through a toll booth and watching his GPS in a car he's worried may break down at any minute.

This is the reality of the young woman who lives alone with tremendous sadness but presents herself as adventurous on her dating- site profile, who smiles anxiously at the cute guy at the gym, and becomes brave when her ex-boyfriend asks if she's seeing anyone.

This is the reality of the woman who gives her testimony joyfully at church but returns home to an emotionally abusive husband whose anger makes her wonder whether she's the "daughter of the King" she's told she is at church or the "worthless bitch" she's told she is at home.

This is the reality of the young student who moves from her socially and ethnically homogeneous small town to a diverse, multicultural university town.

This is the reality of the politician who feels he must separate his "public" views from his "private" views, or the person who feels she can't bring her faith into the workplace.

This is you when you say, "Part of me wants to go conquer that job interview, and part of me wants to stay in bed all day." Or when you say, "Part of me knows it wasn't my fault, but another part of me still feels guilty."

As I've noted, this isn't a *new* reality. Our dividedness is as ancient as humanity's fall from grace. What I would suggest is that the phenomenon of dividedness is more complicated and more pronounced in our globalized, technological age.

I remember going to Disney's Epcot Center when it first

opened. My favorite attraction was Spaceship Earth, a fifteen-minute ride through time that featured humankind's history of communication, beginning with prehistoric humans and ending with a glimpse into the future, when people would be talking to friends on the other side of the world through their televisions. We now live in that future, with Skype, Google Hangout, FaceTime, and myriads of other ways to stay in touch.

Our relational matrix is far larger today than it was prior to the Industrial Revolution and the digital age. We're far more mobile than we used to be: we regularly commute to our workplaces, and we travel globally. We're far more connected through Twitter, Facebook, Instagram, Path, Snap Chat, and online gaming. Our self-worth is primarily tied to "Klout," which is an online way of measuring our influence within our social networks.[21] We're continually assessing ourselves and tweaking our multiple selves in this new matrix of social connections, especially because of the constant barrage of media images of the ideal life and the ideal self. And in the midst of negotiating these many selves, we're quite out of touch with our inner lives.

Are we busier than we used to be? Do we have less time than we used to have? Perhaps not, say the experts. But we *experience* our lives as more fragmented, more scattered, and more divided than ever before. And, pulled in a thousand different directions, we wonder if there is, in fact, a way to freedom.

To Flourish or Not to Flourish

In the coming chapters, we'll learn to pay attention to what's going on within us, not in some narcissistic exercise of self-admiration but in an attempt to cure the narcissism and perfectionism and addiction that plague us. We'll explore further the phenomenon of division, fragmentation, and contradiction that we all experience. We'll look at what some have called the "inner war" that seems to rage between the things we want to do and the things we do, between the people we want to be and the people we are. We'll see how those voices of shame within exist in a complex network of other voices — voices of rage, anxiety, contempt, and willfulness, among others.

And we'll be invited into a life of flourishing, of wholeheartedness, of peace within.

Psychologists and pediatricians sometimes see children who don't flourish — who seem to struggle to gain weight or who experience physical illness or emotional distress. These experts define this condition as *the failure to thrive.* What I see in the lives of so many adult men and women is a kind of spiritual and emotional failure to thrive. Created to flourish, we experience nagging despair. Made to receive and give joy, we battle cynicism and resignation. Invited to relax our control strategies, we anxiously perfect ourselves for others and sometimes even for a God who we believe is eternally disappointed in our lack of progress. We fail to thrive. We fail to flourish.

And yet, beneath the shame, the desperation, the dissatisfaction, and the frantic striving, I listen for the deeper voice, the voice that declares desire — a desire for joy, freedom, flourishing, and wholeness. It's a voice that often remains hidden, buried under cheap, drive-through versions of happiness and perfection. It's a voice we ignore or lose amid the varying selves we mediate in our real and virtual worlds. It's literally aching for expression, but in order to allow that, we often have to deal first with those other inner strangers like shame and disappointment. It takes courage to listen to the voice within.

And so, while this book will be a journey of learning about how we experience the manifold contradictions and complexities of our lives, it will also be an invitation to do the hard work of changing — to pay attention, to listen within, and to see that in doing so, we find what we're actually looking for: the elusive wholeness and freedom for which we so desperately long.

perfecting ourselves to death — and learning to embrace imperfection

Perfectionism is not self-improvement. Perfectionism is, at its core, about trying to earn approval and acceptance.

BRENÉ BROWN

Baseball teaches us, or has taught most of us, how to deal with failure. We learn at a very young age that failure is the norm in baseball, and, precisely because we have failed, we hold in high regard those who fail less often — those who hit safely in one out of three chances and become star players. I also find it fascinating that baseball, alone in sport, considers errors to be part of the game, part of its rigorous truth.

FAY VINCENT, FORMER COMMISSIONER
OF MAJOR LEAGUE BASEBALL

People may spend their whole lives climbing the ladder of success only to find, once they reach the top, that the ladder is leaning against the wrong wall.

THOMAS MERTON

I RAN INTO AN OLD FRIEND and colleague recently who confessed her exasperation with social media.

"I can't seem to crack the Twitter code. It seems like you've got to be wise and witty, bold and discreet. I'm exhausted trying to be what everybody wants!"

I asked her what she'd been writing and blogging about. Her response was quick. "Wholeheartedness!" she exclaimed.

I can relate. Having spent years studying psychology, theology, philosophy, sociology, and more, I sorted through old notebooks, documents, and blogs, looking for the perfect quotes for this chapter. I puzzled over how to best organize it. I wrestled with what the reader would want. Eventually, fatigued and frustrated, I closed my laptop, hoping that inspiration would rise with the sun the next morning.

We are creatures of such complexity that it seems impossible for us to relinquish the need to be perfect. Junkies for approval, we adjust our personal mirrors to reflect back what others want to see in and from us — appropriately modest in church, creative in the kitchen, circumspect at work, compelling in our many presentations of ourselves.

At our disposal is an endless armory of cosmetic weapons to ward off our sworn enemies: failure and disapproval. Self-help books and surgeries, hair color and make-up (which aren't just for women anymore), fitness gurus and life coaches — we're surrounded by aids for the human self-improvement project. Today we can edit pictures on our smartphones by using filters to enhance the present moment. We can delete our inappropriate Tweets and edit our status updates. We can create and re-create ourselves at will.

We turn on our televisions to see the latest iteration of Oprah and her new gurus. We voyeuristically peer into the exotic lives of these celebrities, who talk about creating authentic lives, eating mindfully, and living in the present. And then we tune into the news later on — only to find out that the celebrity guests are being investigated for lying, or cheating, or willfully promoting a product they knew was deficient. Our hopes for self-perfection are dashed when the cruel reality sets in: No one is perfect.

Self-perfection may be an instinct as old as Adam and Eve. From the very beginning, it seems, human beings have been driven to build ladders to heaven. Ashamed of our humanness, we're constantly aspiring to become gods. The relentless drive to perfect ourselves leads to feats of extraordinary achievement.

And utter exhaustion.

The Gifts of Imperfection

I hadn't yet heard of Brené Brown when a client of mine told me to watch a 2010 TED talk she gave. As I recall, I was a bit cynical. When your clients tell you they're learning something profound from someone else, it's humiliating. But it's a necessary humiliation! Those of us who practice as therapists critique abuses of power, but we also love the power we have in the therapy room as the all-knowing experts who help our fragile clients. Recognizing that my client might be able to help me, I checked my ego at the virtual door and opened my Internet browser.

The talk was called "The Power of Vulnerability."[1] I watched it once and haven't watched it since, so I can't recall particular turns-of-phrase at this point. I just remember feeling an extraordinary sense of being known, being understood. Brown put into powerful words my shame, my anxiety, my longing for connection, my desire to be more vulnerable.

Brown isn't a "pop blogger gone viral." She's a researcher who shares her profound insights with great compassion and honesty.

And she makes herself vulnerable in the process, confessing her need for approval, her desire to see all things ordered and right, her compulsive desire to fix and manage and control. She's a kind of modern prophet speaking to an exhausted laity with a message of compassion and, perhaps more importantly, self-compassion.

Her message rings true with so many — at this point her TED talk has been viewed more than 20 million times. And it rings true because it speaks to a place beneath our masks, our defenses, our egos, and our social-media identities. Even the most narcissistic marketing consultant who creates and re-creates identities for a living knows shame, insecurity, and anxiety, even if it's buried a mile beneath bedrock.

What Brown has discovered isn't rocket science. What she's stumbled upon, through listening to numerous stories, is quite clear to those of us who are all too aware of our humanness. "Perfectionism is not self-improvement," Brown declares in her book *The Gifts of Imperfection.* "Perfectionism is, at its core, about trying to earn approval and acceptance."[2] The impact of this quest for approval is severe, a toxin to one's mind and body. As Brown says, "Perfectionism is a self-destructive and addictive belief system that fuels this primary thought: If I look perfect, live perfectly, and do everything perfectly, I can avoid or minimize the painful feelings of shame, judgment, and blame."[3]

There are three extraordinarily important insights we can derive from Brown's research.

First, perfectionism can begin in a very benign way. Each of us, from infancy, looks for the approval and acceptance of our parents. There is no shame in this. We're made to love and be loved, and a deep connection to our parents is crucial for secure relationships in the future. In fact, as neurobiologist Dan Siegel notes, these early connections are crucial for health and well-being.[4] And yet, Brown has found that a craving for approval and acceptance manifesting in perfectionism arises from the soul of an insecure, ashamed person.

This is quite significant. Perfectionism isn't the goal of a proud, puffed-up soul, but of a deeply insecure one. Perfectionism isn't a symptom of pride but of shame and insecurity. It's true that a symptom of perfectionism may in fact be pride: "Can you see how much I'm achieving in so little time?" But the root cause is different.

Second, perfectionism is a toxin. Martin Luther, who led the reform of a duty-driven, works-based, sixteenth-century church, might say, "I said this centuries ago. This isn't anything new." And he'd be right. Brown hasn't stumbled onto a new insight. She's simply connecting research to what we've known for centuries from a variety of sacred texts — with one great exception. Once again, Brown doesn't situate perfectionism within an arrogant human soul, but within a soul with a story of shame and brokenness.[5] As we'll see later, this is both an important psychological insight and an equally important spiritual insight.

The toxic nature of perfectionism is seen in its addictive quality. What we now know about the human brain is this: our choices, though seemingly free, are locked into patterns established early in childhood and grooved into our brains. While our brains are malleable, we simply don't "decide" one day to stop being so perfectionistic and thus relinquish that toxin. Indeed, neurobiologists like Siegel remind us that the enslaving perfectionistic patterns of thinking, living, and relating take years to form and years to be freed from. Given the toxic nature of perfectionism, it's not surprising that Martin Luther's message of grace was so enthralling for his spiritually exhausted sixteenth-century audience. And that Brown's message is equally appealing today.

Third, Brown sees perfectionism as a way of avoiding or minimizing difficult emotions. Perfectionists will often avoid their own feelings of shame and failure by criticizing themselves. The pioneering psychologist Karen Horney writes,

> Perfectionistic persons, as has been said, are deeply afraid of anyone recognizing that their façade is only a façade; hence their madding fear of criticism and reproaches. In this regard their self- recriminations are an attempt to anticipate reproaches and, by raising them themselves, to prevent others from making them — even more, to appease others by demonstrating their apparent severity toward themselves and to elicit reassurance.[6]

Think about it. Before a big presentation, we might say "I hope I don't blow this!" in order to gain quick encouragement from a colleague. Or we'll say "I'm really not sure this will be any good" after carefully preparing a dinner for friends. Horney continues,

> [Perfectionists] feel as if they were living under a suspended sword which may fall down at any moment, although they may not be aware of these fears. They have a fundamental incapacity to face life's ups and downs in a matter of fact way.[7]

In my various roles as pastor, professor, and therapist, I've seen this time and again. I see it when we punish ourselves, and I see it when we punish others. I see it in the burned-out pastor who frustrates his congregation with a demanding moralism but is weary of his own failures and disappointments. I see it in the gifted executive who works more hours than her male counterparts in order to perform well and be seen as an equal. I see it in the young woman who blogs about motherhood, processing her failures as a parent in words, but holding in her fear of being ignored by readers.

Again, the fuel for perfectionism is shame. In shame, we hide our truest, deepest selves, afraid that being vulnerable and revealing these selves to others will lead to failure, disappointment, or rejection. In shame, we compensate by trying to get the love we think we need, the approval we long for, the achievement we hope might bring satisfaction and fulfillment. But protecting ourselves comes at a cost.

As Brown indicates in the title of her best-selling book, it is only by receiving the gifts of imperfection that we can move from the slavery of perfectionism to the freedom of a life of bold risk-taking and courageous love. If we allow ourselves to fall into wholeness, we experience this freedom. But something conspires within us to stay in control so that we don't fall.

The Inner Critic

The Inner Critic conspires to protect us from feeling shame, insecurity, and inadequacy. In fact, much of our busyness can be traced back to the constant frenetic energy we anxiously expend to keep ourselves from feeling shame.

Such was the case for a twenty-something investment banker who put in long hours at work. He'd come to see me in his best business attire, dressing the part but looking worn and weary. Chen was a 1.5 generation Asian-American who desperately wanted to succeed for the sake of his family.[8] By all accounts, he was succeeding. He was making six figures, faithfully attending church, and dutifully caring for his family.

At the same time, Chen was ending work almost every day with a stop at a massage parlor. The guilt and shame he felt about being pleasured by a stranger terrified him, and so he worked harder, putting in even longer hours. But he became more moody, more reactive, and sometimes missed key administrative details that were costly for him and for his clients. He'd never seen a therapist before coming to me. In his culture, it is shameful to be needy in this way. But he came, he said, because the senior pastor of his church, a man he respected, dared to talk about his own fears and insecurities in his sermons.

Chen's courage was remarkable. He began naming the contradictions in his soul. Often he'd say something like "It feels like a part of me is against me, always critical, always telling me to suck it up and be a man." Curious, I'd ask him to give more voice to this Inner Critic. The messages he shared with me were harsh, demanding, even demeaning. Chen was beating himself into emotional submission while climbing the ladder to financial freedom.

Whether we know it or not, each of us has an Inner Critic. Maybe we have more than one. In fact, psychologists have speculated for some time that human beings may have a number of inner voices or sub-personalities.[9] Today there are dozens of works, many of them within the self-help genre, proposing new ways of dealing with that pesky critic inside. Whatever we name it, we need to recognize its reality.

I hear mine almost daily. Right now, it's the voice that tells me my book won't be helpful enough, or that by concentrating on my writing I'm not spending enough time with my wife, or that I'm neglecting a hundred other responsibilities.

It's the voice that tells you you're not attractive enough or successful enough or busy enough, that you're not gifted enough or winsome enough or athletic enough.

It's the voice that led the Reformer I mentioned — Martin Luther — to believe that he wasn't working hard enough to please God.

And it's been whispering in our ear from time immemorial.

The Inner Critic within us takes primary responsibility for keeping us active, on our toes, and hard at work. It plays an important role within, but it can become a harrowing and exhausting bully. Just how does this happen?

If shame and insecurity are a significant part of our childhood story, we're quite likely to develop a strong and loud Inner Critic. This part of us makes sure that the shame story doesn't dominate our lives. It protects us like a police officer might protect a vulnerable child. And, in fact, the Inner Critic is protecting a vulnerable part of us that's afraid to be exposed and be seen.

Much like an overdeveloped conscience, the Inner Critic is determined to keep you from falling, from failing, from disappointing. The critic remembers how it felt for you to be picked last for the kickball team, to be ignored by your alcoholic father, to be pushed hard by your demanding, perfectionistic mother. The critic got in your ear when you were studying for the spelling bee so that you wouldn't experience the shame of misspelling a word in front of your classmates. In fact, the critic's power is so great that many of us still have dreams of forgetting to study for a test or being chosen last for a team. Even our dreams reveal the perfectionistic agenda of the Inner Critic.

The Antidote to Self-Criticism: Self-Compassion

Our tiring attempts to keep life together leave us frazzled and weary. Sometimes we feel torn in two.

Even the towering biblical hero St. Paul knew inner fragmentation:

> I obviously need help! I realize that I don't have what it takes. I can will it, but I can't *do* it. I decide to do good, but I don't *really* do it; I decide not to do bad, but then I do it anyway. My decisions, such as they are, don't result in actions. Something has gone wrong deep within me and gets the better of me every time. (Rom. 7:17-20, *The Message*)

We know just how St. Paul feels because we constantly feel different parts of us pulled in different directions. Today a part of me wanted to wake up, have coffee, and sit on the couch all day watching World Cup soccer. Another part of me reminded myself that I have deadlines — deadlines for this writing project, deadlines for my new syllabi, deadlines for grading a course I'm teaching, deadlines for retreats I'm leading. I let these two parts duke it out for a bit before I settled the squabble. I'd work on my couch with the World Cup playing in the background, and give myself periodic breaks to simply take in the action.

It takes some time to process these inner battles well, and sometimes I lose the fight. But there was a time in my life when that pesky Inner Critic felt more like a bully I always needed to succumb to. When I was in seminary, he whispered in my ear, "You'll never be spiritual enough, Chuck. You've got to pray better and harder." He reminded me that I wasn't getting high enough grades, or attending the premier school, or deserving of a good job. A part of me believed the critic, while another part of me fought back. The resulting fragmentation took its toll.

One toll was panic. My panic attacks began when I was young — perhaps in elementary school — and continued into adulthood. They can still rise up with a vengeance today during times when I'm particularly strained or stressed. Whenever I panicked, the bullying critic would double down: "You see, you're blowing it. You're going to fail, and don't say I didn't warn you!" Exhausted, I'd try harder. Or sometimes I'd simply sabotage something — a test, an opportunity, a relationship.

When I took the risk to get counseling during seminary, the critic chimed in again: "Chuck, you're being silly and stupid. Therapy — really? Just get over it!" And yet, something — some other, deeper voice — told me to stand in the contradictory feelings.[10]

When I started my counseling sessions, I blamed my parents.

42

Therapy often goes in this direction, and it's often necessary to talk about our family of origin and its impact on us with a wise counselor. But sooner or later we realize that Mom is no longer standing over us demanding that we clean our room, and Dad is no longer sighing with disapproval when we can't figure out how to start the mower. In fact, we recognize that the voice isn't outside of us, but within us. It's become integrated into what one writer calls our own "internal family system," the many parts of us that do battle, vying for the lead role in our inner being.[11]

Eventually, we need to address this inner bully. But often we don't. We medicate it. We drink too much to numb its impact. Sometimes we even bless it in the name of some distorted version of religious duty, grateful that we can beat ourselves into obedience. At other times, we name it as an enemy. We may do this in some distorted version of a spiritual warfare theology, believing the voice to be a demon or spiritual menace.[12] Or we may overcompensate with a kind of libertine, throw-caution-to-the-wind approach, saying, "I don't need rules and responsibilities and duty. It's my life, and I'll do what I want!" But treating the Inner Critic as an enemy only serves to empower it more.

So, how do we address this Inner Critic? Researchers are discovering that compassion is the key.

University of Texas professor Kristin Neff, like Brené Brown, devotes her life to understanding our complicated lives. And, like Brown, she believes that we're exhausting ourselves by attempting to perfect ourselves.

In her best-selling book *Self-Compassion,* she argues that our fixation with perfection begins at an early age.[13] In today's success-and-happiness-driven culture, we push our children to be the best while at the same time we fear letting them in on the great truth — that perhaps they're not. Believing our children will be ill-equipped to thrive without constantly hearing about how special or wonderful they are, we set them up for disaster. We prime their Inner Critics with fodder for a later date, when they'll tell these poor children that, in fact, they're quite incompetent and need to try harder. The self-esteem movement, Neff contends, might actually be contributing to our perfectionistic neuroses.[14]

Think about it. All around us are messages of exceptionalism. We hear our president talk about American exceptionalism. We see our children's classmates get awards for exceptional behavior or performance. We see our compulsively hard-working cube-mate be praised for doing an exceptional job. And we watch the ads on TV that give us pictures of exceptional meals, exceptional bodies, and exceptional vacations. Immersed in this culture, we strive to be exceptional too.

And in an attempt to boost the egos of our children, we create little narcissists who strive to be all-powerful but hide their deep insecurity behind a thousand masks. Afraid to fail and disappoint, they pretend until they can't pretend anymore. That's often when I get a call.

Like the call I got from Jack, third in a line of "Jack's" and heir to the family company. Jack was pushed hard to succeed in school and in sports. The implicit message was clear: *If you fail, the family fails.* He was also reminded each and every day of his family name — the name on billboards and in commercials and on the stock exchange. Called to be exceptional, Jack played the role — football captain, star student, teacher favorite. Until Jack stole money from the family business.

The response from Jack's family was quick and severe. Jack was no longer the heir apparent; his family distanced themselves from him, privately hoping they could endure the wave of media criticism. When Jack finally came to see me, he felt lost and abandoned. The once-confident man who'd appeared smiling in his father's commercials was the tarnished prodigal son. And when he and I began to talk, years of hidden shame came pouring out.

Jack was done avoiding his shame. He walked into it, through it, within it. He asked big questions of it, and came to understand both his story and his heart better. A year later, Jack felt free. Although he had spent several months in prison, he now called his former life a prison. He started a landscaping company, something he'd secretly longed to do but was never allowed to dream about. He loved the outdoors, the smell of fresh-cut grass, and the freedom from his toxic family expectations. And when he had a son, he named him Paul, not Jack.

Still, it took Jack years to become free from the lingering inner voice that would remind him that he was a failure, a disobedient son who'd embarrassed the family and spoiled the dreams of his parents. Jack and I spent time working with that Inner Critic. And what he learned, over time, was not to ignore it or fight it, but to listen to it.

When Jack was a boy, the Inner Critic served as a strong ally, helping him to avoid the wrath of his father and the disgust of his mother. But in his teenage and college years, the Inner Critic became fierce. Fearing possible failure, the critic spoke harshly.

But Jack redefined this relationship as he and I worked together. Sometimes Jack would imagine his Inner Critic seated in a chair next to him. Compassionately, he'd ask, "Why so angry? Tell me what you've been through." And to his amazement, the critic would respond. He learned that his seemingly critical enemy was actually a friend, a part of himself that grew to protect him from the judgments of his parents.

Listening to the critic's experience, he spoke internally to it, saying, "You seem really tired."

"Yes I am," he heard his inner companion say.

This began a new, ongoing dialogue that brought greater wholeness. Jack could approach himself, and others, with compassion.

Compassion is a kind of antidote to perfectionism, a response to ourselves that breeds greater wholeness and deeper rest. It comes from our less reactive, higher brain, giving us the capacity to love and empathize. Neff writes,

> Compassion is, by definition, relational. Compassion literally means "to suffer with," which implies a basic mutuality in the experience of suffering. The emotion of compassion springs from the recognition that the human experience is imperfect.[15]

The Inner Critic, on the other hand, is connected to our brain's threat mechanism, a reptilian holdover from millennia of self-protection in the face of danger. It views life through a reactive lens.

Importantly, Neff and others argue that self-compassion is far more crucial to our well-being than self-esteem. Self-compassion is the practice of an imperfect person, someone who is *merely* human in an age when we're all trying to be superhuman. Self-compassion allows us to give ourselves the gift of being adequate at many things instead of exceptional at everything. Self-compassion gives our Inner Critic the day off. Self-compassion frees us from the slavery of narcissistic self-promotion and self-perfection. Self-compassion frees us to pay attention to the inner conversations we're always having, as we debate which voice will decide the moment, the day, the future. Self-compassion allows us, in the end, to be imperfect.

Embracing Imperfection

When Bill Wilson, the founder of Alcoholics Anonymous, proclaimed *powerlessness* to be a first principle of recovery, I'm quite certain he offended his mover-and-shaker friends. Wilson's first step in his well-known twelve-step program proclaims what all of us fear greatly — that we are powerless and unable to manage our lives on our own. And his belief that we find salvation in a Higher Power is an attack on the gospel of exceptionalism, self-sufficiency, and perfectionism.

In their book *The Spirituality of Imperfection,* two of Wilson's disciples tell stories of inadequacy, disappointment, failure, imperfection, and humanness. This text is by no means a "Christian" one. It champions a kind of secular spirituality, testifies to a human instinct recognized by a variety of traditions and cultures. In this context, even Fay Vincent, a former Commissioner of Major League Baseball, gets to weigh in:

> Baseball teaches us, or has taught most of us, how to deal with failure. We learn at a very young age that failure is the norm in baseball, and, precisely because we have failed, we hold in high regard those who fail less often — those who hit safely in one out of three chances and become star players. I also find it fascinating that baseball, alone in sport, considers errors to be part of the game, part of its rigorous truth.[16]

This truth became real for me just two nights ago. I play softball for the Pillar Church team. Twenty years ago I was a pretty good hitter. Today I'm mediocre, and that troubles my perfectionistic soul. But in this recent game I started out well. In my first at-bat, I hit a clean single past the shortstop, and felt pretty good. I followed it up with some great base-running, which my teammates cheered with some surprise, as if they were thinking, *He may be better than we realized.*

And then I blew it. I got caught between second and third base in a rundown and was tagged out. Humiliated, I grabbed my glove to wait for the end of the inning. Minutes later, I found myself under a routine fly ball to right field. My anxiety shot up as the ball was in flight, but I caught it — a small victory. But then I grounded out in my next two at-bats, ending the night with one hit, multiple bouts of anxiety, and a sense that I'd failed the team.

And then the coach walked by and said, "Nice job, DeGroat — a hit, a walk, great on-base percentage. We need that." In my mind, I'd failed the team by not getting on base every time. But according to the coach, I'd beaten the odds.

In fact, I had matched Fay Vincent's statistics, going one for three. In baseball, this is the norm. In life, this is unacceptable. And so many of us fear not doing everything perfectly.

As a consequence, we live anxious lives. And we live busy lives. Afraid of our humanness and the shame that comes with an honest recognition of it, we devote our anxious energy to our self-improvement projects. Instead of embracing our normalcy and perhaps even our mediocrity, we strive to achieve. We put in the extra hours at work to gain our boss's approval. We follow our to-do list for fear of being seen as lazy, incompetent, or inadequate. We stretch our narcissism muscles in an attempt to be all things to all people: omnipotent, omniscient, omnipresent — inhuman!

Thomas Merton writes, "People may spend their whole lives climbing the ladder of success only to find, once they reach the top, that the ladder is leaning against the wrong wall." You probably know couples who've been married for fifty years and praised for their long-lasting union even though they're long-suffering and miserable. You probably have a wealthy friend who lost his wife and children during his climb to the top of the wrong wall. And you probably know about the megachurch pastor who preaches love and harmony but whose life at home is in ruins. Clearly, we'll do a lot to protect ourselves from the dread of imperfection and failure.

But what if imperfection was, in fact, a gift to be embraced rather than an enemy to be thwarted? What if our humanness was a kind of grounding principle that anchored us to earth despite our attempts to climb the ladder to heaven? What if through — not despite — our imperfections we were falling into the very wholeness we'd sought? What if we lived with greater curiosity about every part of us that remains divided?

The incapacity to extend compassion to ourselves condemns us to a life of dividedness, fueling the Inner Critic's internal dictatorship and shame's perpetual self-condemnation. Blocked from the love we need from others and from God, we remain enslaved to our guilt, our failures, and our imperfections. But if we can become capable of a gracious compassion that reaches to every divided part of our being, we can become capable of living whole and holy lives.

With a poet's voice, Elsie Landström hints at the wholeness and holiness that arises when we welcome every divided, messy, imperfect, ugly, and critical part of ourselves into the embrace of grace:

Over the years I have caught glimpses of you
in the mirror, wicked;
in a sudden stridency in my own voice, have
heard you mock me;
in the tightening of my muscles felt the pull
of your anger and the whine
of your greed twist my countenance; felt your
indifference blank my face when pity was called for.
You are there, lurking under every kind act I do,
ready to defeat me.
Lately, rather than drop the lid of my shock
over your intrusion,
I have looked for you with new eyes
opened to your tricks, but more,
opened to your rootedness in life.
Come, I open my arms to you also, once-dread stranger.

Come, as a friend I would welcome you to stretch your apartments
within me from the cramped to comforting side.
Thus I would disarm you. For I have recently learned,
learned looking straight into your eyes:
The holiness of God is everywhere.[17]

What might it mean for us to consider welcoming every
stranger within us? How might it change the way we live and work
and relate if we freely embrace, rather than fight, parts of ourselves
that whisper messages of shame and criticism?

Landström suggests that we might find more than ourselves —
that we might also find God. That may just be too much to handle
at this point! So while we turn our attention to the human brain
and its dividedness, let's also imagine, if only briefly, a world in
which God might be found in the parts of ourselves we consider
most imperfect. If we can begin to do this, we might be taking our
first steps toward the elusive wholeness for which we long.

using our brains:
the neurobiology of wholeness

The busy lives people lead in our technologically driven
culture that consumes our attention often produce a multi-
tasking frenzy of activity that leaves people constantly doing, with no space to breathe and just be. The adaptations
to such a way of life often leave youth accustomed to high
levels of stimulus-bound attention, flitting from one activity
to another, with little time for self-reflection or interpersonal connection of the direct, face-to-face sort that the
brain needs for proper development.

DANIEL SIEGEL

The intuitive mind is a sacred gift, and the rational mind is
a faithful servant. We have created a world that honors the
servant, but has forgotten the gift.

ALBERT EINSTEIN

Whole people see and create wholeness wherever they
go; split people see and create splits in everything and
everybody.

RICHARD ROHR

"JUST GET SOME REST," my pastor told me many years ago when I came to him as an anxious and somewhat despairing young man. He told me to exercise, start each morning with Scripture, and focus less on my problems. He proposed a kind of distraction therapy in which I would ignore my troublesome feelings by engaging in supposedly helpful and healthy activities.

His advice was immediately gratifying, because I felt empowered. *I can control this,* I thought. And his advice was logical. It made sense to do things which would take the focus off my problems. And so I did what he said.

Yet just a few months later I nearly drove my car off the road in an act of despair and self-sabotage.[1] Was my pastor wrong? Was his counsel poor? In fact, I think it was fairly true to the dominant paradigm available to pastors then and even to therapists today, a way of viewing human beings that reduces us to rational, decision-making machines subject to simple processes of change. This mechanistic model, a product of the Enlightenment, is only a few hundred years old. It assumes that with clear reason and sound observation, one can figure out and fix any malady.

In this chapter, I argue that the latest brain research tells a different story. I turn my focus to the human brain, exploring compelling research that shows the complexity of our psyches. I look at the impact of this "split-brained" thinking on human life, and its potential to inflict more — not less — exhaustion, fragmentation, and suffering. And in doing so, I show how counsel and care are affected when human beings are reduced from mystery to machine. Throughout the chapter, we'll see the surprising impact of brain science on our everyday battles with busyness and perfectionism.

The Story of Splitting

Why we do what we do is a great mystery. If only it were as easy as observing a behavior and naming a motive for it! And yet, with St. Paul we might say, "I do not understand what I do."[2]

Indeed, we now know enough about the human brain to know that it takes many years to connect the disparate dots of our lives. Many of our life experiences lead us to places of disconnection, disharmony, and dividedness. The best psychology and neurobiology show us that the quality of our earliest relationships goes a long way toward setting up our brains to thrive.[3] Our developing brains try to make the best sense possible out of the many wild and wonderful events of our early days, including Uncle Jake's funny but disturbing "silly faces" and Grandpa nearly dropping us when we were two months old and Mom not responding as quickly as we would have liked for the next feeding.

Our earliest memories are implicit memories, stored in a variety of areas in the brain. These memories aren't organized like many of our later memories. They're not narratives with a definite "me" involved. We can't place these memories on a neat timeline and give them a definite plotline. In fact, our early emotions and perceptions and bodily traumas are actually encoded in patterns or schemas that impact the way we view the world and relate to others later in life.

Some early life experiences are quite frightening or traumatic, so much so that our brain finds a way to protect us from what's happening. These experiences may involve a natural disaster, a crime, an act of sexual abuse, or the violent rage of a parent, among many others. The memories of these events, just like those of more benign experiences, are encoded implicitly. A child who was touched inappropriately may "remember" that event in a part of her body; a child who witnessed a crime may "remember" it in a headache or a panic attack. At a functional level, however, the memory is split off, stored in the unconscious, until something or someone triggers it later.

Judy experienced a dramatic triggering event when she was just fourteen years old. It was the Fourth of July, and just after she was tucked into bed, an extremely loud firework woke her. She froze, and her tense body made her look comatose. When her mother checked on her just minutes later, she screamed for her husband to call an ambulance, sure that her daughter was dying.

Why did this happen? The loud firework triggered an implicit memory dating back to Judy's first months of life, a memory Judy had no conscious recollection of. When she was two months old, a gas line in her neighborhood burst near her home as Judy's mother was feeding her. Her mother was so alarmed that she accidentally flipped Judy onto the floor and under a dresser. Judy's mother and father were grateful that she was unhurt, and they assumed that she was so young that she would never remember the incident. But in fact she did: the implicit memory was encoded in a particular part of her brain, and was "recollected" in the "firework" moment. Even so, Judy wouldn't make this connection for nearly two decades, because her mother and father treated the firework event as a false alarm. They never sought help for Judy's extreme reaction or talked with Judy about it after that night.

Judy's story is a very dramatic one; most of our stories are less so. But the same processes are at work in all of us. For example, most First-World children learn at a very early age that hard work and good behavior are important. We're told to stop fussing while Mom is checking out in the grocery line, and we're scolded for incessantly whining and nagging when our parents are busy cleaning the house for an evening gathering. These are fairly typical stories — but even these are internalized in ways that create patterns or schemas for future behavior. Consequently, as adults we might feel anxious or angry as we wait in a long grocery line with a slow checker. We might be short with our spouse or frustrated with ourselves as we frantically scramble to clean our home before friends arrive. Our spouse might say, "Why do you get so uptight about these things?" But we don't know. We just do.

We certainly aren't conscious of it, but we're operating out of long-held schemas. And we may have developed various strategies for protecting ourselves. When we're hurt or relationally dismissed or scolded or abandoned, we might tuck more than memories away — we might tuck parts of ourselves away. These parts, like certain memories, are "split off," fragmented from our consciousness.

The parts of us that split off are called "Exiles" by psychologist Richard Schwartz. And the parts of us that rise up to survive our difficulties are called "Protectors."[4] Each of us, according to Schwartz, navigates life in a way that best helps us to survive given our unique circumstances and psychic composition. However, as our compensatory "Protectors" doing their inner juggling interact with the hidden "Exiles," we can find ourselves out of sorts in a way that we describe as fragmented or torn.

Trauma or abuse need not be the cause of this. In fact, our lack of inner integration can occur through seemingly normal activity. Daniel Siegel describes how today's young people suffer in this way:

> The busy lives people lead in the technologically driven culture that consumes our attention often produce a multitasking frenzy of activity that leaves people constantly doing, with no space to breathe and just be. The adaptations to such a way of life often leave youth accustomed to high levels of stimulus-bound attention, flitting from one activity to another, with little time for self-reflection or interpersonal connection of the direct, face-to-face sort that the brain needs for proper development. Little today in our hectic lives provides for opportunities to attune with one another.[5]

And this accurately describes not just youth — it describes us adults too. As we live divided and fragmented lives, we reveal something about our brains. What neurobiologists tell us is that this is a sure sign that some sort of developmental process or set of experiences has occurred which has rendered us dis-integrated. Wholeness can come only through an intentional process of mindful re-integration, a process we'll explore later. For now, though, let's explore yet another aspect of our dividedness.

The Battle between the Left and the Right

At some point in elementary school, we all learned that our brain was, at the very least, split in two. Perhaps we heard generalizations like this: *The right side of your brain is creative and artistic, and the left side of your brain is logical.* This was the classic position, in fact, and few of us are aware that it's been contested. In recent times, however, this quick-and-easy explanation has been dismissed by brain researchers who dispute the traditional two-hemisphere theory in favor of a more integrated theory. Their take is that both sides of the brain are involved in our many activities, from logical thought to artistic creation to intuitive connection. Few today would disagree that both sides of the brain are involved in all of our many activities. Both the left side and the right side are engaged in language, engaged in reasoning, and engaged in creating. This is a crucial insight.

However, Iain McGilchrist's extraordinary work, *The Master and His Emissary,* has reframed this debate, adopting the new perspective with a twist. He writes,

> My thesis is that for us as human beings there are two fundamentally opposed realities, two different modes of experience; that each is of

56

ultimate importance in bringing about the recognizably human world; and that their difference is rooted in the bihemispheric structure of the brain.[6]

In other words, while both hemispheres are engaged in our many activities, they're engaged in different ways. The right hemisphere sees context, while the left hemisphere focuses in with precision. The right makes big connections, while the left makes careful and logical observations. The right holds paradox, while the left chooses sides. As McGilchrist writes, "So the left hemisphere needs certainty and needs to be right. The right hemisphere makes it possible to hold several ambiguous possibilities in suspension together without premature closure on one outcome."[7]

This is quite an extraordinary thing if, in fact, the two hemispheres are lovingly and cooperatively dancing together. Sadly, though, the left hemisphere tends to hijack the process. Armed with its precise rationality, it convinces us and the world of its superior importance. And we, who long for certainty and precision and clarity in times that are uncertain, join Team Left Hemisphere. The tragic outcome is a brain — and, by extension, a society of people — that is polarized.

Albert Einstein anticipated this when he said, "The intuitive mind is a sacred gift, and the rational mind is a faithful servant. We have created a world that honors the servant, but has forgotten the gift."[8] The servant, our logical left hemisphere, takes an increasing meaning-making role in our thinking, our feeling, and our willing. So the once-cooperative duo of left and right find themselves embroiled in a struggle for power. And instead of valuing both important contributions, we live from the hemisphere we think will give us the advantage.

It has been greatly beneficial to human beings throughout history to have both a more intuitive, artistic hemisphere and a more logical, precise hemisphere. The delicate balance allows us to both enjoy a sunset and understand the phenomenon of the earth's rotation. This balance gives us the freedom to fall in love while at the same time making the very rational decision to leave the one we love because he is abusing us. But at certain points in history, McGilchrist contends, the left hemisphere becomes the dominant hemisphere both personally and societally:

> I suggest that it is as if the left hemisphere, which creates a sort of self-reflexive virtual world, has blocked off the available exits, the ways out of the hall of mirrors, into a reality which the right hemisphere could enable us to understand. In the past, this tendency was counterbalanced by forces from outside the enclosed system of the self-conscious mind; apart from the history incarnated in our culture, and the natural world itself, from both of which we are increasingly alienated, these were principally the embodied nature of our existence, the arts, and religion. In our time each of these has been subverted, and the routes of escape from the virtual world have been closed off. An increasingly mechanistic, fragmented, decontextualized world, marked by unwarranted optimism mixed with paranoia and a feeling of emptiness, has come about, reflecting, I believe, the unopposed action of a dysfunctional left hemisphere.[9]

The fascinating and important insight for busy, exhausted people like you and me is this: While we've looked to our left brain for the insights we need to progress and grow, we have — quite unwittingly — succumbed to its most negative aspects: its propensity for division, fragmentation, expediency, and certainty. As a people, we're feeling the emptiness that comes when our attempts at control are thwarted. And instead of embracing our "other half" with renewed vigor in an attempt to hold life's paradoxes and navigate its perplexities, we've recommitted to mastering life — controlling, competing, and expediting. We're constantly searching for the latest techniques, gadgets, and insights to give us that elusive control we long for.

And it's not working.

Minding Our Inner Terrain

When we consider our extraordinary complexity, "the brain can be seen as something like a huge country," writes McGilchrist: "as a nested structure of villages and towns, then districts, gathered into counties, regions, and even partly autonomous states or lands."[10] Daniel Siegel views it as a vast sea. He writes,

> Within each of us there is an internal mental world — what I have come to think of as the sea inside — that is a wonderfully rich place, filled with thoughts and feelings, memories and dreams, hopes and wishes. Of course it can also be a turbulent place where we experience the dark side of all those wonderful feelings and thoughts — fears, sorrows, dreads, regrets, nightmares. When this inner sea seems to crash in on us, threatening to drag us down below to the dark depths, it can make us feel as if we are drowning. Who among us has not at one time or another felt overwhelmed by the sensations from within our own minds?[11]

As we reflect on Siegel's description, perhaps we're inclined to agree. In just a matter of moments, we can feel many different things. Triggered by a comment from our spouse, we may feel both ashamed and angry. Waiting for the last out of the World Series, we might be filled simultaneously with anxiety, ecstasy, and dread.

And these feelings may evidence themselves physically. Our sweaty hands express our anxiety; our red face shows our shame; our constricted throat betrays our panic; our clenched jaw holds our rage. While a surge of reactive anger might swell in our gut, it may be opposed by an equal and opposite rational thought in our minds that cautions us to remain civil.

In short, we are multifaceted beings who experience shifting thoughts and feelings. And we're always shifting and changing to meet the challenges of life. We show up to work as our competent selves, to the party as our crazy selves, to the counseling session as our vulnerable selves, and to church as our polite and put-together spiritual selves.

We'll explore this multifacetedness more fully in Chapter 8, but here it's important to recognize a significant insight offered by neurobiologists: To the extent that we ignore our vast inner sea with all its diversity and complexity, we inflict our dividedness on others. As Franciscan priest and author Richard Rohr writes, "Whole people see and create wholeness wherever they go; split people see and create splits in everything and everybody."[12] In other words, paying attention to what's going on inside is crucial for wholehearted living and flourishing relationships.

Think about it. When you and I lack self-awareness, we inflict our enraged self on a co-worker or our avoidant self on our spouse. Or we unwittingly project our unresolved anxieties onto our children, who then internalize the divide themselves. Unaware, we simply react to life's situations rather than reflecting on what we're feeling and where we are and what we need. In fact, if we've never learned to listen to our hearts, we might be completely unaware of our unique stories, our manifold feelings, and the state of our relationships.

When we live reactively, we're prone to merely survive rather than to thrive and flourish. Consider the story of an angry, exhausted young woman I saw for counseling some time ago. Denise was in her late twenties and working part-time while living with some good friends. Her job wasn't difficult: she simply answered phones for a local company, taking messages and forwarding calls.

In her spare time, she exercised, attended a church group, and ran a variety of errands. And yet, when she came to see me, she described her life as exhausting, overwhelming, and impossible to manage. She told me she had alienated friends at work and at church because she was "constantly on edge" and "didn't want to be bothered by their crap." What she wanted from me were some simple time-management strategies, and maybe a few Bible verses to help with the anger.

She was a bit perturbed when I chose a different approach, asking about her upbringing and her relationships. Her responses showed no self-reflection; she'd simply say, "It was fine" or "I don't see why that's relevant." Soon enough, she began responding, "If you're wondering if my parents were bad, they weren't. We had a great family." But our process had already begun to unearth feelings she hadn't acknowledged before. At first she recognized some sadness. Then she acknowledged anger. And during our sixth session, she put words to her deep feeling of shame as she covered her face and shed tears. In the beginning these emotions felt like uninvited strangers, but over time she began to acknowledge and welcome them, learning what she could with curiosity and compassion.

As her capacity for self-reflection grew, she noticed reactive patterns of responding in her work and her relationships. One major insight came when she recognized how tense she was each day at work. Largely out of tune with her own body for years, she'd gone to a chiropractor for pain relief, but she hadn't considered the anxiety permeating her entire being. She made real progress when she began noticing the shame that existed beneath the anxiety, accompanied by a voice she recognized as her mother's, saying, "Denise, you're a disappointment." That was her pervasive reality as a six-year-old.

Imagine the impact of those words on a young child. And their resonance continued, like waves pulsing through her vast inner sea, impacting her and those around her.

Anxiety and shame became millstones around Denise's neck, making her feel much older and more tired than she should have. In her constant state of low-level anxiety and despair, she'd react angrily to almost everyone around her. But this began to change when she did her inner work and better understood her own story.

According to Siegel, minding our inner terrain involves a process of integration that requires us to cultivate an inner curiosity and awareness. But this requires intentionality, time, and space, gifts we rarely give ourselves. Denise came to me because she wanted a time-management tool. What she ultimately came to see was that she needed to use the time she had to cultivate an inner attention, a mindfulness. I remember the eye-opening embarrassment she felt as we walked through her schedule together and noted the many opportunities she had for intentional self-reflection. I recall the relief she felt as she began to let go of addictive patterns of watching too much television, mindlessly searching for random things on the Internet, or simply living "checked out," as she called it. And in the process she recognized the wide-open spaces she had to attend to her inner life.

As Denise grew in her capacity for mindful self-awareness, she became more patient with herself, despite the nagging inner voice of disappointment. She received grace from herself and from others. In her new freedom, she felt less compelled to mindlessly watch TV or "numb out." In fact, she cultivated practices that employed her whole self, her whole mind, her whole being, and she felt truly alive and genuinely present in her own life.

I remember the joy she experienced when she discovered a new hobby — cooking — which allowed her to cultivate presence and join it with curiosity and desire in order to engage something new, creative, and life-giving. A year after we'd begun therapy,

Denise was no longer looking for time-management skills. She was a winsome display of wholeness and life. No longer exhausted, she pursued graduate education in the culinary arts, and is now a chef. Denise is a picture of wholeness, a picture that illustrates what leading neuropsychologists and biologists are saying about brains that function holistically.

Living a Whole-Brained Life

"Use your brain!" my older daughter cried out impatiently to her younger sister when they were just six and four. My wife was attempting to home-school them then, and Emma, who was older and a bit overconfident in those days, couldn't understand why Maggie wasn't excelling at the same level she was.

Use your brain.

If only it were that easy. If only our brains were computers that could be accessed on demand and modified at will.

What neuropsychology shows us with great clarity is that we're not flying solo. We're embodied, relational people whose lives and minds are connected to those of others. Our divisions emerge from the inner divisions of our parents and extended family, our early peers, and our developmental successes and failures. Where we bring our inner divisions, others experience division. Where we bring our wholeness, others experience wholeness. This is a kind of "law of nature," or perhaps a law of the brain, which ought to give us pause and humility as we consider our relationships. Denise is a good example. At some level she experienced the inner divisions of her mother and internalized those divisions herself. And without some hard work on her part, Denise would still be perpetuating divisiveness — unwholeness — in her relationships.

Neurobiologists are teaching us much about division, both

within and without. What we come to see through the important insights of neurobiological research is that even our small squabbles actually reveal something about our capacity, or lack thereof, for wholeness and integration. We reveal our dividedness when we're triggered and react suddenly and harshly to a friend. We reveal our neural disconnects in the ways in which we fight. We display our left brain/right brain imbalance in our passionate defenses of certainty or ambiguity. Our political, social, and theological wars say more about our psychic divisions than they do about real differences.

It takes great humility to become self-aware, for what we see we might not like. But self-awareness or mindfulness is the first step toward change, toward wholeness. Our brains are malleable, capable of adjusting to new realities. So we need not remain in our reactive patterns. When we notice them, we can admit that we're stuck, and, after doing some hard inner work, we can move on.

One of the great insights of brain science in the last forty years that enriches our understanding of personal and social dividedness is the concept of the triune brain. It was the innovative thought of a neuroscientist named Paul MacLean in the mid-1960s. Psychiatrist Curt Thompson explains the model of the brain that MacLean developed:

> He termed the model the triune brain, based on his observation that the human brain seemed to function as three interwoven brains in one. In MacLean's model, the brain consists of the reptilian complex, the limbic circuitry, and the neocortex.[13]

The evolution of the triune brain is a story too substantial to tell in this summary section, but I'll give a quick overview of it here, because it's yet another fascinating conception of our brain. It explains how we get stuck in reactive patterns. It shows our propensity to live our lives in highly functional ways, yet with little self-awareness. It reminds us how we fail to use our (whole) brain.

In the triune brain, the reptilian brain is our most fundamental brain, the center of our fight-or-flight responses, responsible for our quick reaction to a bug about to fly into our eye or a car about to hit us. It's our oldest brain, and it kept us safe in hard times, just as it does today. Like an inner policeman, it reacts quickly to ward off threats. It's our inner Jason Bourne, constantly scanning for danger. It's a critical system, but if we lived out of it alone, we'd have few friends.

The limbic system, according to Thompson,

> . . . is largely responsible for recognition and memory of fear, attention to salient internal or external environmental stimuli, and pleasure. This area of the brain relates to the generation and modulation of emotion. It is the wellspring of primal neural activity that eventually emerges, once processed in the cortex, in the form of fear, joy, disgust, anger, hurt, disappointment, relief, and dozens of other emotions. It is highly connected by nerves to the other two parts of the brain to assist in the modulation of both the higher (cortex) and lower (brainstem) activities of the brain.[14]

The most well-developed system and the one that makes humans unique is the neocortex. It enables us to love with a self-giving love, to discern our unique vocational inclinations, to write a poem, to envision a way to attain peace in the Middle East. It's our reflective brain, and it shouldn't surprise us to learn that we don't harness its remarkable gifts often enough.

Of course, we get through life on the helpful functions of the first two systems. We'd hardly get along without the seemingly automatic promptings of our lower brain, which enable us to breathe, to pump blood, to acknowledge the urgent pressure on our bladder, and to avoid a fastball aimed at our skull. Yet we're made for so much more. The neocortex may literally be calling to us in times of reactivity and division, saying, "Slow down. Think and reflect. Be attentive to what's really at stake!"

Armed with some basic insight into how our brains work, we can see how we can quickly fall victim to our reptilian fight-or-flight responsiveness in an argument with our spouse, rather than "leaning in" and allowing ourselves to move into a more elevated conversation. We can see how we react, even at a national level, in times of crisis with knee-jerk responses ("Our response will be swift and severe") rather than thoughtful ways of engaging. Indeed, in much of life we're interacting with people who are addicted to reptilian-brain thinking, or inordinately attuned to left-brained mechanical and logical responses that avoid ambiguity and uncertainty. And particularly in times of crisis, both personal and corporate, we're almost automatically inclined to reactivity rather than reflection.

Consider Denise again. When she came to see me, she was living her life by accessing the first two regions of her brain. Her reactivity and exhaustion were a kind of default mode. In a sense, someone needed to tell Denise to "use her brain" because, in fact, she hadn't learned the astounding art of self-reflection.

My work with her was fairly straightforward. Without her knowing it, I asked her to access her higher brain. I did that by asking her to begin to reflect, to notice emotions, sensations, feelings, images, and more. Although she initially reacted and resisted, defaulting back to her older, lower brains, she eventually allowed her highly evolved neocortical brain to engage, and something within her changed. She began to own her life story and make sense of it. She felt more present, more engaged. And she relaxed. She became a different person by taking the courageous step of moving beyond reactive fight-or-flight patterns and into wholeness and wholeheartedness.

What we're learning from those studying the brain is that we're quite capable of living whole lives if we engage our entire brain. My daughter Emma was right after all — we need to use our brains! Our right brain holds the gift of seeing the big picture, of connecting the dots, of sensing the beauty of life. Our higher neo-cortical brain holds the gifts of mindfulness and self-awareness, which develop our capacity to reflect rather than to react. It is indeed glorious that we're not merely machines to be reprogrammed, but wonderfully complicated people endowed with complex brains capable of solving difficult puzzles and writing beautiful poetry.

In the next section, we'll discover our capacity for greater wholeness as we exercise different parts of our brains. We've done some analyzing, and we've assessed some of the research from 50,000 feet. Now we'll explore more deeply the resources of our higher neocortical brain, discovering a larger language for our inner divisions through poets and priests, monks and mystics. Let's invest our whole hearts (and whole brains!) as we engage every part of ourselves with great curiosity for the sake of wholeness and wholeheartedness.

Part 2

AWAKENING TO WHOLENESS

CHAPTER 4

awakening to our lives: a poetic invitation

One day you finally knew
what you had to do.

MARY OLIVER

What I do is me: for that I came.

GERARD MANLEY HOPKINS

Give wine. Give bread. Give back your heart
to itself, to the stranger who has loved you.

DEREK WALCOTT

AS WE'VE DISCOVERED, life pulled in a thousand different directions breeds exhaustion, reactivity, and dividedness both within and without. Pulled to and fro, we lose connection to our hearts. We lose touch with the present moment. We react anxiously. We get stuck in patterns that suck the life out of us — and those around us.

In the previous chapters, we've heard from neurobiologists and brain scientists, from psychologists and sociologists. But in this chapter we turn our attention to poets, mystics, and wise souls, women and men who model wholehearted living for us.

Poets call us back to the only life we have to live — our own. Pulled in so many different directions, we often feel we're living someone else's life, someone else's agenda, someone else's dream. We can become emotionally detached from our work, "phoning it in" and praying that the weekend comes quickly. We can sleepwalk through life, half-heartedly participating in it, depriving those we love of our full presence. Sometimes we feel as if we're living to meet the expectations of others — a spouse, a boss, a parent, a client — and we lose touch with our own longings and dreams and desires.

Poets invite us to wake up.

Waking Up to Our Lives

Mary Oliver has become a favorite poet of mine. Her poem "The Journey" was an early source of grace during a time of near-burnout in my ministry.

I recall feeling like I was doing everything I could possibly do and still letting everyone down. I was a pastor, a therapist, a clinical supervisor, a part-time professor, and I was trying to work on a Ph.D. My meetings with others were always full and felt heavy, as I'd bear the stories of hurting men and women. My job required me to be fully present, to listen well and ask good questions.

And I was praised for my availability and my compassion. People needed me, and I was there for them. I was there when a client was in need, when a student wanted to talk, when a faculty meeting was called, when my Ph.D. advisor had a question.

But a significant part of me began to resent others. Perhaps you've experienced this. You begin to dread opening your e-mail. You ignore phone calls. You look in the other direction as people walk by. You avoid people you view as needy or helpless. And yet you're stuck fighting the guilt that comes when you let someone down.

For me, help came in the form of Oliver's poem:

One day you finally knew
what you had to do, and began,
though the voices around you
kept shouting
their bad advice —
though the whole house
began to tremble
and you felt the old tug
at your ankles.
"Mend my life!"
each voice cried.
But you didn't stop.
You knew what you had to do,
though the wind pried
with its stiff fingers
at the very foundations —
though their melancholy
was terrible.
It was already late
enough, and a wild night,
and the road full of fallen
branches and stones.
But little by little,
as you left their voices behind,

the stars began to burn
through the sheets of clouds,
and there was a new voice
which you slowly
recognized as your own,
that kept you company
as you strode deeper and deeper
into the world,
determined to do
the only thing you could do —
determined to save
the only life you could save.[1]

As the poem begins, you feel the pressure, the pressure we all experience sometimes when people tug at our ankles and cry, "Mend my life!" Maybe it's the cry of a needy child, or an exacting boss, or an impatient customer, or a room full of demanding elementary students. In the past, you've just given in, perhaps reluctantly, perhaps resentfully. You've come through. You've failed to disappoint.

But this time is different. This time you realize something greater is at stake: your life. You've failed to nourish the very life that serves as a conduit of grace to others.

"One day you finally knew," says Oliver. What makes this day different than any other is a mystery. Maybe on this day you've awakened to the depth of your own needs. Or maybe you're just sick and tired of living someone else's life, completely out of touch with your own. Maybe you felt that your health was suffering, or, like me, you found yourself on the edge of burnout. Whatever it was, "You knew what you had to do."

You knew. You knew it couldn't continue. You knew you'd burn out or explode or hurt someone if you continued.

You knew — and yet this doesn't make the road ahead easy, as Oliver makes very clear. The road back into your own life, your own heart, and your own health can be a treacherous one. Oliver uses vivid imagery to illumine the obstacles — the stiff wind, the terrible melancholy, the late hour, the wild night, the dangerous road.

Oliver underscores the truth that fighting for and finding your own life is dangerous and difficult. Much has happened in your life to create detours, division, and distance from your own self and others. Society, your psyche, and your brain conspire in their division-making work. Becoming whole is a journey, a risky one, a "wild night."

In the Christian contemplative tradition, this wild night is "the dark night of the soul," as the sixteenth-century poet St. John of the Cross called it. It is the night that strips you of everything that is not you. It is a gift, God's gift. It is God's way of exposing every mask, every false self, every protective layer that keeps you from living your life whole and holy. In the dark night, you become aware of your addictive need to come through for others at the cost of your own heart. You see the idolatry of usefulness and helpfulness and the esteem you get from being the hero. You see how far you are from living from your deepest core, from a place of longing and desire.

But soon enough, the dark gives way to the light:

> But little by little,
> as you left their voices behind,
> the stars began to burn
> through the sheets of clouds,
> and there was a new voice
> which you slowly
> recognized as your own. . . .

When I lived in San Francisco, the sun would slowly burn away the insistent fog, revealing a deep blue sky and the bright yellow ball of hot energy that, oftentimes, found itself a stranger to chilled city-dwellers. Likewise, something deep within you burns through the exhausted false selves to reveal your truest self. You know it when you meet it. You might say, "There you are! I've missed you."

This journey isn't narcissistic or purely therapeutic or simply for you. As Oliver says, the new voice keeps you company as you do what you must: save the only life that you can save. This new voice, which is your own, is the only voice capable of loving others. It is *you,* your deepest self, freed from your enslaving false self, and capable of authentic and sincere compassion. It is you, whole and holy.

What I find remarkable about this poem, as I revisit it time and again, is Oliver's trust in a certain inviolable human attribute — the true self. This is the self capable of loving others, of experiencing resilience in the face of shame, of reflecting calmly in the middle of a difficult experience.

Of course, Oliver admits that there's a certain hiddenness we experience, seen in moments when we're simply reacting to the next thing in life. But she is full of hope that we're capable of living beyond our false selves.

Still, sometimes we feel that sense of being trapped in an inescapable prison, unable to get outside ourselves, unable to free ourselves from the obsessive and compulsive thoughts and activities which exhaust us. Sometimes we're so exhausted that we're not sure who we are or what we want. Though we long for the grace that Mary Oliver offers us, sometimes the division within feels permanent.

The twentieth-century Chilean poet Pablo Neruda finds himself there. He writes,

Of the many men whom I am, whom we are,
I cannot settle on a single one.
They are lost to me under the cover of clothing.
They have departed for another city.

When everything seems to be set
to show me off as a man of intelligence,
the fool I keep concealed on my person
takes over my talk and occupies my mouth.[2]

Is there any hope for those of us who feel unable to break free from our false selves — exhausted, compulsive, perfectionistic, hopelessly helpful, driven, and divided?

Seeing the Light

The Quaker spiritual writer Thomas Kelly gives me hope.

He reminds me that there is something more, something more to me than my compulsions and obsessions, than my despair and discontent.

He says that there is a treasure buried deep within my heart and yours, buried beneath a hundred false selves, an inextinguishable Inner Light. He reminds me that I am more than a "triune brain," more than the sum of my divided parts, more than my obsessions, more than my perfectionism. But it takes *spiritual* insight, according to Kelly, to see this Inner Light.

"The secular mind," Kelly writes, "is an abbreviated, fragmentary mind, building only upon a part of man's nature and neglecting a part — the most glorious part — of man's nature, powers, and resources." This "secular mind," resigned to what can be seen and measured, disallows the possibility of spirit, of soul, of the true self. On the other hand, Kelly notes, "The religious mind involves the whole of man, embraces his relations with time within their true ground and setting in the Eternal Lover."[3]

Kelly invites us to have the eyes to see that we are rooted and grounded in something deep and lasting. As we are pulled to and fro, he invites us to look within, to see the brightness and feel the warmth of the Inner Light, God's anchoring presence.

Kelly trusts that this Light and this Life within speak, even beckon, beyond our conscious recognition:

> He who is within us urges, by secret persuasion, to such an amazing Inward Life with Him, so that, firmly cleaving to Him, we always look out upon all the world through the sheen of the Inward Light, and react toward men spontaneously and joyously from this Inward Center.[4]

Kelly believes that we are always being pulled back to our Center, despite our attempts to run from it. Our distractions won't have the last word.

When we awaken to the Life that flows within like a deep river, we become attentive to our true self and our true vocation. It is as if the weight of keeping our lives running is lifted, and we see — finally — who we truly are and what we're called to become. In the midst of his own relational and vocational emptiness, the philosopher Søren Kierkegaard heard this quiet, inner beckoning, and it became a prayer: "Now, with God's help, I shall become myself."[5]

This same confidence is echoed in the beautiful words of the Jesuit priest and English poet Gerard Manley Hopkins. He believes that to find our true vocation, we must first find ourselves. And, in finding ourselves, we find the Inner Light, which is Christ living in us:

> Each mortal thing does one thing and the same:
> Deals out that being indoors each one dwells;

Selves — goes itself; myself it speaks and spells,
Crying *What I do is me: for that I came.*

I say more: the just man justices;
Keeps grace: that keeps all his goings graces;
Acts in God's eye what in God's eye he is —
Christ — for Christ plays in ten thousand places,
Lovely in limbs, and lovely in eyes not his
To the Father through the features of men's faces.[6]

What Hopkins proposes may at first seem absurdly selfish: *What I do is me: for that I came.* And yet for Christ to play in ten thousand places, we must find him in us first. For the plumber to plumb and the gardener to garden and the priest to pastor, she must first discover that deepest vocation in her being, the deepest self beneath the many imposter selves.

Taking the First Step toward Wholeness

In "Love after Love," the poet Derek Walcott paints an extraordinary picture of one who discovers this Inner Light, who awakens to her deeper life and celebrates the homecoming:

The time will come
when, with elation
you will greet yourself arriving
at your own door, in your own mirror
and each will smile at the other's welcome,

and say, sit here. Eat.
You will love again the stranger who was your self.

Give wine. Give bread. Give back your heart
to itself, to the stranger who has loved you

all your life, whom you ignored
for another, who knows you by heart.
Take down the love letters from the bookshelf,

the photographs, the desperate notes,
peel your own image from the mirror.
Sit. Feast on your life.[7]

Walcott envisions a feast, a celebratory feast. Employing the language of the Christian Eucharist, he imagines a kind of Holy Communion which is, in fact, a holy reunion with our deepest self. He imagines you and me feasting on our own lost and hidden lives, awakened to that deep hunger, that strong inner current we so often ignore.

For Walcott to imagine this reunion, he must know the path of dividedness, of exhaustion, of perfectionism. He must know the daily realities that enslave us. He sees the bills that keep us up at night, the mortgage we can't afford, the overtime we take because every last dime counts. He sees our lifeless faces as we sip coffee on our morning commute. He sees the disgust in our eyes as we walk by our boss's office. He hears the apathy in our voices as we speak to our spouse on the phone. He knows our way of reactive, reptilian-brain living. Walcott sees our lives of quiet desperation. And yet in this poet we see the belief that something more beautiful and life-giving resides within. Walcott believes that we can awaken to our own lives and greet the stranger who looks us in the mirror.

I hear many men and women say to me, "I don't even recognize myself anymore." I hear it from women who are a hundred pounds over their preferred weight. I hear it from addicts who continue to revisit their bone-dry wells. I hear it from the underemployed and the over-achieving. And I find myself asking them, "Who are you? Tell me."

It's terrifying to hear someone say in response, "I don't know." I'd rather believe that he chooses not to, or that perhaps life has conspired to fog the windows and block the radiant Inner Light.

I've come to believe that there is, in fact, a Spirit that dwells within us. God takes up residence. The Inner Light conquers our darkness, and cannot be extinguished. And recognition of this Inner Light is the first sacramental step on the road to wholeness and wholeheartedness.

Glimpsing the Beautiful Freedom of Wholeness

Prompted by ads and prodded by our spouses, we look to the latest and greatest techniques to prop up our aging bodies. We put on masks at an early age, but we make them increasingly sophisticated over time. The fig leaves that cover our shame inevitably wither and fall away, and so we create more elaborate coverings. And the marketplace is glad to comply with our wishes for the newest and the best — and the best-looking.

Because we're not awakened to our truest selves, we live out the stories of others — our cultural idols, our icons. *Please make my hair look like Jennifer Aniston's. Please let me look like George Clooney when I put on a suit.* We're all looking for a better life to live, a prettier shell to show the world. And it's exhausting us.

In churches I've served, I've known people who hope that grace will propel them into their "best life." Though attracted to church because of the offer of grace, they quickly put on a new mask, a religious one, which helps delete from memory any foibles and fumbles. Let's face it — we'll do just about anything to edit our stories. We'll find whatever makeover works best, whether religious or social or vocational or cosmetic. I know this from painful personal experience.

The New Zealand poet Fleur Adcock teaches me something about true beauty and grace in her poem "Weathering." Her words penetrate my vanity, which only fuels anxiety, shame, and more exhaustion. It makes me wonder if I can truly feast on my life, as Walcott says, or recognize my own voice, as Oliver insists. Because so much in life conspires against this authenticity; so much blocks the Inner Light.

For Adcock, it's the beauty of a place that awakens her to the Inner Light. I've heard different theories about the particular place that captures her imagination, but it doesn't really matter where it is. Beauty can awaken us wherever we find it, whether we're strolling through a wooded canopy or driving along the ocean cliffs in California or watching a sunset over Lake Michigan.

Hemmed in by cubicles and suburban jungles and trapped in cars, we're unable to see the beauty through our bleary, weary eyes. When I lived in San Francisco, my own daily commute took me through the Marin Headlands north of the city and over the Golden Gate Bridge. People save for a lifetime to visit San Francisco, and this was my personal playground. Still, there were many mornings when I was oblivious — tuned in to sports radio or engrossed in some anxious preparation for the day — and I missed the great beauty that surrounded me in every direction.

Adcock is a poet-prophet who reminds me to look again. She paints an astounding picture of a life that is possible, a life of wholeness, in which one can simply *be who one is.*

My face catches the wind
from the snow-line

and flushes with a flush
that will never wholly settle.
Well, that was a metropolitan vanity,
wanting to look young forever, to pass.
I was never a pre-Raphaelite beauty
and only pretty enough to be seen
with a man who wanted to be seen
with a passable woman.

But now that I am in love
with a place that doesn't care
how I look and if I am happy,
happy is how I look and that's all.
My hair will grow grey in any case,
my nails chip and flake,
my waist thicken, and the years
work all their usual changes.

If my face is to be weather beaten as well,
it's little enough lost
for a year among the lakes and vales
where simply to look out my window
at the high pass
makes me indifferent to mirrors
and to what my soul may wear
over its new complexion.[8]

The grace that Adcock extends to herself is overwhelmingly attractive to the driven, cosmetically modified, insecure man or woman who knows the "metropolitan vanity" of which she speaks.

Adcock tried a thousand different outfits in front of the mirror before choosing one — which, as it turned out, was the wrong one.

She did the dance between curling iron and flat iron. She tried Weight Watchers and the Paleo Diet.

But then she discovered beauty. We're not told how or where. I once had a friend who moved to Montana to find beauty only to finally discover it in a life-giving conversation on the flight back home. Beauty always surprises us. And that's the way it's supposed to be. But when the Inner Light comes flooding out, we know it, and we soar into the transcendent. Listening to Adcock, we feel as if she's been there:

> But now that I am in love
> with a place that doesn't care
> how I look and if I am happy,
> happy is how I look and that's all.

And that's all.

She could have ended the poem there, and we would have envied her definitive arrival. In fact, we might have idealized it. But as she continues, we're plucked out of our romanticizing and brought back into reality. She talks about her greying hair, her weakening nails, her thickening waist.

This is what we didn't want. This is what we've exhausted ourselves trying to avoid. Adcock's details penetrate our own vain selves. We see how hard we've worked to fight nature, to resist God's time-tested ways of aging us.

We realize that our exhaustion comes in part because we've made aging the enemy. Instead of battling against inauthenticity or fragmentation or disconnection in ourselves, we've conspired with all of them to fight with our very selves. When we do this, we block the Inner Light and become unable to see what's most beautiful within us and around us.

What if we, like Adcock, could become "indifferent to mirrors," to what our souls wear on the outside? We might grow in our capacity for wholeness and holiness. We might actually become *who we already are,* anchored in Love.

As it turns out, our soul's journey to self-discovery isn't at all narcissistic. What is narcissistic is our exhausting, self-sabotaging life of perfectionism, whether we pursue it through financial success or religious ritual or even finding God's perfect match for us.[9]

What the poets we've explored agree on is that we're hidden to some degree — hidden behind false selves who make us strangers to our true selves, hidden behind fig-leaved garments that veil our shame and insecurity and anxiety. We're hidden, and we're exhausted. Deprived of the wholeness for which we've been made, we settle for half-lives.

But perhaps today is different. Perhaps we've gotten a hint, heard a whisper, seen a glimpse of that Inner Light. Perhaps today is that day when, to paraphrase Mary Oliver, we know what we need to do.

Wholeness, according to the poets, begins when we start listening to our lives, paying attention to our deepest desires and abandoning all of our self-improvement projects, even the particularly religious ones we believe will make us who we think we should be. Free from the "other lives" we've been trying on like garments off a rack, we can greet the stranger who is our true self and live from the Inner Light. And perhaps, in time, we'll experience the freedom of Fleur Adcock, whose holy indifference to mirrors allows her the grace to live her own life and let that be a nourishing gift to others.

If it could only be! But there are so many obstacles to wholeness — even religious ones. How we can overcome them is what we'll focus on next.

becoming holy without becoming exhausted

Who shall ascend the hill of the LORD?
    And who shall stand in his holy place?
Those who have clean hands and pure hearts,
    who do not lift up their souls to what is false,
    and do not swear deceitfully.
They will receive blessing from the LORD,
    and vindication from the God of their salvation.

PSALM 24:3-5, NRSV

Holiness, as taught in the Scriptures, is not based upon knowledge on our part. Rather, it is based upon the resurrected Christ in-dwelling us and changing us into His likeness.

A. W. TOZER

May God himself, the God who makes everything holy and whole, make you holy and whole, put you together — spirit, soul, and body — and keep you fit for the coming of our Master, Jesus Christ.

ST. PAUL, 1 THESSALONIANS 5:23-24, *THE MESSAGE*

O F ALL THE DIFFERENT KINDS of exhaustion we experience, the most fatiguing of all may just be spiritual exhaustion. It's hard enough to please a boss, a client, even a spouse. But pleasing the Divine — well, that can seem almost impossible.

People often say to me, "You speak a lot about wholeness. But doesn't the Bible focus on holiness?" Behind this question I hear the subtle voice of the Inner Critic lurking, whispering, "Surely there is more to do — more prayers to say, more discipline to enforce, more progress to make."

And so we're driven to excel, to ascend, to climb the religious ladder up into the holy of holies. Indeed, no matter the religious tradition, some sort of ascent into the holiest of places seems required for spiritual maturation. Progress is reserved for the dedicated, the devoted, the disciplined. Purity is reserved for the set apart, those who've managed to flee every kind of evil that might corrupt, those who've risen beyond "earthly" things. Those who do attain holiness are seen to be saintly, to have a kind of ethereal and other-worldly countenance that reminds the unholy of their remaining imperfections.

But what if holiness was more like the elusive wholeness that we've been considering? What if spiritual maturation was not so much about ascent but about descent — about falling into wholeness? What if purity was about union and not about separation? What if holiness was available to all, and not merely to the select few conquerors of sin and the devil?

The Exhausting Climb

Mired in guilt, a single mother confessed that she hadn't prayed in weeks. A young deacon confessed lustful thoughts. A woman on food stamps shared her battle with envy. Each had made their way to church to get right with God. But even after inspiring sermon and song, each returned to their spiritual angst after the service.

Echoing in their ears was part of the Psalm read that morning:

> Who shall ascend the hill of the LORD?
>> And who shall stand in his holy place?
> Those who have clean hands and pure hearts,
>> who do not lift up their souls to what is false,
>> and do not swear deceitfully.
> They will receive blessing from the LORD,
>> and vindication from the God of their salvation.

Who shall ascend? Certainly not the prayerless single mom. Certainly not the lusting deacon. Certainly not the envious woman on the brink of poverty.

While most Bible readers probably don't spend vast amounts of time reading the Old Testament book of Leviticus, they can tell you what it's about. To most, it's about sacrificing, abstaining. It's also about defiling, desecration, defectiveness, consecration, dishonor, disgrace, uncleanliness, guilt, and the law. They can tell you about it because they live it every day, feel it every hour. They can tell you about it because despite promises of grace and love and wholeness, it still feels like their God is waiting above, ready to pounce at the first hint of guilt.

When we are unable to ascend, guilt and shame take up permanent residence in our inner being. The Inner Critic stands guard vigilantly, eager to remind us of the slightest infraction. Our minds churn over our most recent or vivid violations, while our spirits sink, fatigued by our lack of progress.

Who may ascend? Certainly not you. Certainly not me.

Have you experienced this fatigue? Have you had moments of spiritual panic when you realized you don't make the cut? Have you fallen on the way up the holy mountain? I have. And I haven't stopped falling. And this is the story of countless others I've spent time with over the years. They talk of distance from God and spiritual dryness and uninspiring devotions and snail-paced progress. Some of them talk about God feeling like an unsafe father who abandoned them long ago and whose stern look makes them wonder if they could ever please him.

Who may ascend?

When we look around, we think we see a few. They tend to look and dress the part in their fancy vestments and Christian executive suits and expensive holy-hipster jeans. They carry leather-bound Bibles and never seem to frown. Their certainty makes us quiver every time we doubt. They can ascend, and after a close assessment of their spiritual Boy Scout badges, God can receive them with a "Welcome, my good and faithful servants."

This is how many of us view holiness.

On a retreat I was part of recently, a debate started about how Christians grow. A few made the standard claim: "God saves us by grace." But one participant said what many were thinking: "That's fine, but after God says 'Not guilty,' he expects us to prove him right."

Our versions of holiness often mean precisely that: *We need to prove God right.*

So for many of us, believing is exhausting. This is precisely why spiritual leaders are observing a precipitous decline in worship-service attendance. Religion is a dying business. Most people are still interested in God, but not in all the baggage that seems to come along with belief.

But I'm hoping that maybe we've missed something. That's because I don't want to abandon faith. Maybe I'm naïve, but I can't quite get on board with the therapeutic gods of today who simply seek my own good. That story feels all too convenient, and I'm not convinced that convenience is the mark of the great religious traditions. And these are my questions: Is holiness about ascent? Is it about getting our acts together and climbing the holy mountain? Is it about setting ourselves apart and banishing every blemish? Or is there a different way of telling the story?

An Unholy Reversal

It must have startled the young fisherman named Peter when Jesus came along one day and said, "Follow me" (Matt. 4:19). Imagine the fierce response of Peter's Inner Critic: "Me? Are you talking to me? I'm just a lowly fisherman, stuck here because I don't make the cut in your religiously buttoned-up society. You've got the wrong guy here."

The scene here is startling and counter-intuitive. First of all, gods don't come down to earth unless they're on a seek-and-destroy mission. And second — and more important — the Divine doesn't mingle with unworthy souls. Why on earth is Jesus mingling with commoners like Peter?

It is the perception of many that in the Judeo-Christian tradition, God takes great care to make sure we know who the insiders and the outsiders are. Careful rules establish who we may and may not mingle with. And perhaps the most significant rule of all is this one: that we may not dare enter God's holy presence, let alone "mingle." Only one man, the High Priest, would be allowed to do this, once a year on Yom Kippur, the Day of Atonement, and not without blood sacrifice (Heb. 9:7). The message seems clear: Getting an appointment with God is rare, and comes at great cost. And the conversation isn't casual.

But when an unworthy tax collector named Matthew re-writes the script in the very first book of the New Testament, he indicates from the outset that something new is going on. He starts with a genealogy, indicating a kind of "new Genesis" or new beginning, one that evidently includes unworthy women, and even women who were prostitutes.[1] And this new beginning will feature the promised one called "Emmanuel," a name which means "God with us" (Matt. 1:23). Evidently this God is interested not only in including us but in re-connecting, in being with us.

In order to remind his readers that the previous Story isn't irrelevant, Matthew goes to great lengths to show how this promised one, Emmanuel, must go through the same initiatory pattern that ancient Israel did — persecuted by a ruthless dictator (compare Exodus 1:8-14 to Matthew 2:13-18), targeted in a crusade against innocent infants (compare Exodus 1–2 to Matthew 2:16-18), rescued and reminded of true identity (compare Exodus 19:5 to Matthew 3:17), exiled into a wilderness (compare Exodus 13–40 to Matthew 4:1-11). And this God-among-us is evidently interested in choosing the not-so-qualified to serve, just as he did with Israel.[2] As I re-read the Story, I wonder if I've missed something about holiness.

I think back to the prophet Isaiah, the prophet who I was told was most concerned about holiness. Every time I hear the hymn "Holy, Holy, Holy," I think of him, stunned into silence by this holy-and-separate God. But here too, I'm stunned as I re-read the Old Story I've been told time and again. When I focus on Isaiah 1, I can't get any further than this:

> Quit your worship charades. I can't stand your trivial religious games: Monthly conferences, weekly Sabbaths, special meetings — meetings, meetings, meetings — I can't stand one more! Meetings for this, meetings for that. I hate them! You've worn me out! I'm sick of your religion, religion, religion, while you go right on sinning. When you put on your next prayer-performance, I'll be looking the other way. No matter how long or loud or often you pray, I'll not be listening. And do you know why?

Because you've been tearing people to pieces, and your hands are bloody. Go home and wash up. Clean up your act. Sweep your lives clean of your evildoings so I don't have to look at them any longer. Say no to wrong. Learn to do good. Work for justice. Help the down-and-out. Stand up for the homeless. Go to bat for the defenseless. (Isa. 1:13-17, *The Message*)

My historically and culturally assumed notions of holiness don't hold up when I begin to see this New Story unfolding. Maybe yours don't, either. But it takes a bit more investigative work for me.

In what seems to be a climactic moment in an unholy reversal, Jesus ascends a mountain just as Moses did and invites his friends up with him. The symbolic moment must have been thick with intrigue and great curiosity as the young men and women following Jesus scratched their heads in confusion while making their way to his perched pulpit. Just imagine what they were thinking: *What will he say? What demands must we meet? What will this "New Moses" ascending the mount command of us?*

The Way Down Is the Way Up

With his listeners expecting some divine pronouncement about holy and righteous living, Jesus begins in a way that must have raised eyebrows, inspired chuckles, and incited fury: "Blessed are the poor in spirit, for theirs is the kingdom of heaven" (Matt. 5:3).

The poor in spirit?

Amid suspicious whispers, some must have wondered if God-with-us might be God-the-Fraud. The poor, or *ptochos* in Greek, are those who've hit bottom, those who've come to the very end of themselves, those whose relentless working hasn't worked. The poor are unworthy, unholy, marginalized, and labeled. They are wanna-be citizens living on the border and young black men gunned down in the streets and those deemed sexually impure who are asked to check their perverted baggage in the church lobby.

The poor in spirit? Really, Jesus?

Holiness is cast in a very different light at the outset of the Beatitudes, and it only gets worse for readers hoping that Jesus will course-correct. We're awakened to the reality that our maturation process isn't about perfection. Rather, our holiness and wholeness mean "embracing brokenness as an integral part of life," says Parker Palmer. "Knowing this gives me hope that human wholeness — mine, yours, ours — need not be a utopian dream, if we can use devastation as a seedbed for new life."[3]

I don't know about you, but I was hoping that God wouldn't use my devastation as the seedbed for new life. I didn't want devastation. I wanted holiness. Progress. The upwardly mobile Christian life. I wanted people to tell stories of my great sanctity.

But then I read what Dominican father Simon Tugwell writes about the Beatitudes:

> Blessed are the poor in Spirit, those who have allowed themselves to be stripped of the old spirit, the spirit of acquisitiveness and security, because theirs is the kingdom of heaven, because they no longer seek to possess but to be possessed, to lose themselves and all that is "theirs" in the ecstasy of simple receiving and simple giving again, or, more accurately, without even any giving or receiving, in the simple being which is the authentic image in us, that divine ecstasy of being which is the living God.[4]

For Tugwell, becoming poor in spirit strips us of everything that is *not truly us*, bringing us back to the "simple being," God's "authentic image in us." Becoming poor strips us of our inner divisions, including the spiritual masks we've worn in the exhausting holiness game we've been playing. This is crucial, Tugwell says, because we cling to our falseness:

Like runaway slaves, we either flee our own reality or manufacture a false self which is mostly admirable, mildly prepossessing, and superficially happy. We hide what we know or feel ourselves to be (which we assume to be unacceptable and unlovable) behind some kind of appearance which we hope will be more pleasing. We hide behind pretty faces which we put on for the benefit of our public. And in time we may even come to forget that we are hiding, and think that our assumed pretty face is what we really look like.[5]

It is precisely this spiritual inauthenticity that Jesus preaches against, aiming his harshest criticism at the supposed holiest-of-all, the Pharisees, calling them "white-washed tombs" and "play-actors" (Matt. 23:27) who've taken the spiritual stage at the expense of their wholeness and, consequently, their holiness.

For Jesus, the way of ascent is the way of descent.

Read that again: The way of ascent is the way of descent.

Utterly counter-intuitive. Paradigm-shifting. This is the kind of stuff that gets people in trouble. And Jesus would soon discover that reality.

To drive home the point of his sermon, Jesus ramps up the rhetoric:

Blessed are those who mourn, for they will be comforted.
[*Read:* Lament. Grieve. Get it all out.]

Blessed are the meek, for they will inherit the earth.
[*Read:* Be humbled. Let that ego shatter.]

Blessed are those who hunger and thirst for righteousness, for they will
  be filled.
[*Read:* Long more deeply than you've ever longed before.]

Blessed are the merciful, for they will receive mercy.
[*Read:* Let yourself be moved by and for the other.]

And then Jesus says, "Blessed are the pure in heart, for they will see God."

And perhaps we overhear a conversation:

"Purity in heart. There it is — the holiness the righteous ones have been looking for. Perhaps this Beatitude will make sense of all the others!"

The Wholeness of Holiness

"Blessed are the pure in heart," Jesus says, "for they will see God." People have been trying to "see God" for ages. As the Story goes, human beings have been hidden from God since time immemorial, cast out from the primordial Garden, doomed to build towers upward into the clouds and ladders into heaven to try to ascend into the holy place.[6]

The exhausting upward climb didn't lead to holiness or intimacy or even wholeness. It seems to have led to the kind of stage play at which the religious elites of Jesus' day became adept. It certainly didn't lead to "purity of heart," the language Matthew ascribes to Jesus in this instance.

Again, the original language is telling. Purity, or *katharoi* in Greek, is about a state of being, about a fundamental undividedness or wholeness that marks the life of *shalom*. It flies in the face of the dividedness of religious leaders like the Pharisees, who cleaned themselves up and separated themselves from the so-called sinners but ended up impure, divided, and hypocritical. Purity is about being put together again, being made whole, so that our inner life matches our outer life. As it turns out, it's not about some exhausting holiness project; it's about letting God do the purifying work through our brokenness, mourning, meekness, hunger and thirst, mercy, and more. It's about surrendering our clean-up acts and allowing God to do the deep cleansing.

How do we make sense of this when it seems that everything we've been taught drives us into perfectionistic holiness projects?

As I muse on the entire story line of the Bible, it seems to me that the Story can be told *this* way. Humankind, made to see and know God in beautiful intimacy, betrayed that gift. Originally entrusted with *shalom,* a glorious flourishing and wholeness, humanity instead chose hiddenness, dividedness, and self-protection, which was manifested in a fig-leaf wardrobe (Gen. 3:7) that has adorned us ever since. We all hide. None of us is immune. Our fig leaves come in many shapes and personalities — proud, confused, angry, critical, abandoned, comical, nice, fun-loving.

In the Judeo-Christian story, God's rescue plan involved choosing certain people to become bearers of his wholeness and holiness once again; they were to be the ambassadors of this wholeness and holiness to the world. God chose Noah. Abraham. Moses. Israel. David. And in a hundred stories less well-known, he chose the seemingly unworthy ones — people like Rahab and Tamar and Ruth. God's rescue plan, as I often like to say, involves our taking baby steps back into God's presence. The "law" becomes that baby-step tool. The laws says, "You've learned to disrespect important things like people, boundaries, food, land, holy days, and even me. I'm going to be your teacher." God's rescue plan involves choosing a people and giving them a way back into God's presence, symbolized in the Old Testament in the tabernacle and the temple. After making a people whole and holy, God would send them out to show others the way.

But, as it turns out, the so-called chosen ones took the law to be the end-game, the goal, the means of displaying their supposed purity and exposing the impurity of others. In doing this, they became the "hypocrites," betraying the very whole-and-holy project they'd signed up for. They made purity about an outward appearance, a false self, and by doing so they split us into two, into three, into a hundred fragmented pieces. Fractured and divided, we stumble our way around, choosing whatever path seems to lead up to the holy place.

This is why God *comes.*

Emmanuel, God-with-us, comes down to meet us in our despair, our exhaustion, our shame. God bears it all — shame, humiliation, persecution — because this holiness-and-wholeness project is worth it, because we're worth it.

But as Jesus makes clear in the Sermon on the Mount, it comes at great cost to our control strategies, our ego games, and our holiness projects. God in Jesus seeks to free us from the burdening chains of the exhausted false self, saying, "Take my yoke upon you, and learn from me; for I am gentle and humble in heart, and you will find rest for your souls. For my yoke is easy, and my burden is light" (Matt. 11:29-30). God isn't interested in exhausting us. Maybe that's why Jesus calls his message "Good News."

But the "good news" pathway requires some significant heartwork. This is why Jesus says, "Blessed are the poor in spirit." We learn from the next Beatitudes that we must lament. And be humbled. As we can see, becoming whole isn't about applying a cosmetic strategy. It isn't about beefing up our holiness credentials. We do literally fall into wholeness and holiness when every aid we've used to hold ourselves up is knocked out from under us.

And what we learn is that those who are whole become ambassadors of *shalom,* of wholeness. Jesus says, "Blessed are the peacemakers, for they will be called children of God." What Jesus is saying is this: *Blessed are those who call forth shalom, flourishing, and wholeness in this broken and divided world.*

Those who call for peace, for union, and for wholeness will know that wholeness because they'll be reminded, in their inmost being, that their identity is as children of God — beloved, belonging, believed in.

And these are the kinds of men and women who might find themselves persecuted (Matt. 5:10-12). After all, isn't that what happens to those who risk living wholeheartedly in a broken world?

Finally, as Jesus concludes his sermon, he reminds his listeners that his ambassadors will become like "salt" and "light," light for a "city on a hill," radiating a message of wholeness amid division, healing amid broken-heartedness, union amid separation.

Perhaps, along with those young men and women listening intently, we find ourselves wondering if this God-with-us Messiah can bring about the promised *shalom* we're all expecting.

Removing Every Obstacle to Union

Can this kind of Messiah bring peace? Can he possibly address every division, both within us and among us?

It seems that Jesus was concerned about removing every obstacle to union with God, both in us as individuals and in our communities. Jesus longed to see every source of division destroyed. He entrusted a large part of that mission to St. Paul, who writes,

> But now in Christ Jesus you who once were far off have been brought near by the blood of Christ. For he is our peace; in his flesh he has made both groups into one and has broken down the dividing wall, that is, the hostility between us. He has abolished the law with its commandments and ordinances, that he might create in himself one new humanity in place of the two, thus making peace, and might reconcile both groups to God in one body through the cross, thus putting to death that hostility through it. So he came and proclaimed peace to you who were far off and peace to those who were near. (Eph. 2:13-17)

Those of us who are pure in heart become peacemakers, bringing about *shalom* on the inside and the outside. We become ambassadors of wholeness, naming the divisions and calling for union. And whether the names have been St. Augustine or St. Theresa, Martin Luther King Jr. or Brené Brown, the task has continued and will continue.

Jesus makes it clear that the whole-and-holy life will require some hard work on our part. He doesn't hand us a self-esteem booklet. He doesn't give a you-can-do-it motivational speech. Jesus asks men and women to take out the scalpel and apply it to themselves in an act of major heart surgery.

How do we do this? Removing every obstacle to union first requires us to see that we harbor internal obstacles, parts of ourselves that act out of accord with our deepest, truest self. Identifying and naming these divided parts is a first big step to moving toward wholeness. But this is quite difficult, particularly for those of us who'd rather blame others for our perpetually divided lives.

Many years ago, the seminary that I attended identified a campus-wide issue. This shouldn't have been a surprise, but it was reported as one. In a memorable moment that I still reminisce about with friends, a seminary leader got up to speak, identifying *lust* as the major issue and naming the easy access to pornography as a major culprit. Red-faced, most of us (who were young men at the time) got the message once-and-for-all when this leader exclaimed, "Stop it!"

To aid our obviously weak and undisciplined souls, seminary leaders distributed a memo to the women studying at the school at the time, kindly asking them to "button up" in order to prevent men from stumbling. As I recall, the women I knew were furious. One friend said to me recently, "It was as if they were saying, 'This is your fault, women!'"

Jesus would beg to differ. On lust, Jesus is merciless. He exclaims,

> You have heard that it was said, "You shall not commit adultery." But I say to you that everyone who looks at a woman with lust has already committed adultery with her in his heart. If your right eye causes you to sin, tear it out and throw it away; it is better for you to lose one of your members than for your whole body to be thrown into hell. And if your right hand causes you to sin, cut it off and throw it away; it is better for you to lose one of your members than for your whole body to go into hell. (Matt. 5:27-30)

In this case, the scalpel is out. Perhaps Jesus might even suggest the use of a chainsaw. In his typically hyperbolic and compelling way, Jesus is telling us to do the hard work on ourselves.

This is the point that the hypocritical Pharisees missed. They didn't see that finger-pointing only creates more division and polarization, never leading to wholeness, holiness, or unity. Jesus makes the same point about anger, oath-taking, and retaliation. Over and over again, Jesus asks us to take a good long look within. The real obstacles lie there, not in the heart of the other.

In my work, I often ask people to do this hard work of applying the scalpel. I ask them to look hard at their own stories, both how they've been hurt and how they've hurt others. I ask them to name parts of themselves that are triggered, often in our meetings together, and frequently when strong, triggering emotions arise. I ask them to transcend their reptilian brains and their black-and-white-certainty left-brains and become reflective. This is very difficult work. Often the pain gets worse before it gets better.

One young man who was depressed at first resisted this hard work. He wanted me to ascribe his depression to brain chemistry, his mother, and a difficult series of romantic relationships. He wanted someone to commiserate with him, not to act as a "peace-maker" in this important moment in his story. But, even though we did acknowledge the impact of difficult relationships and get him the important anti-depressant medication he needed, I refused to stop there. We continued the difficult process of exploring his inner world until we stumbled onto a very lost little boy hiding inside of him.

Hidden behind rage and numbing depression, this little boy had no chance of coming out and speaking. But because this young man did the hard work of heart surgery, we were able to get into deeper places still, the well-source of symptoms. He called this part of himself a little boy because in his body it felt very, very young, and very fragile. Initially he balked a bit, citing the "stupid psychological bullshit" of inner children, but I assured him that I wasn't going down some esoteric psycho-babbling rabbit hole, and that I was quite curious about whatever the very young part of him wanted to be seen and known.

I'll never forget him saying, "He's all alone."

I asked him, "So a very significant part of you has been all alone and felt all alone for a long time?"

He nodded, and in tears he joined me over the next twenty minutes of our session, curiously exploring this lost part of himself. Somehow he'd always known it was there. But he had coped by engaging in exhausting spiritual disciplines or frantic busyness or, most recently, enduring burdening depression.

"It's like this part of me is saying that we've been alone for a really long time," he told me.

Together, in the sacred and holy space of that therapy room, we weren't concerned about fixing it or figuring it out. We were concerned about what this very young part of him needed, and most of all how it needed the love of God.

I said to him, "This is why God reveals himself as Father or

Mother, as older brother or as compassionate Spirit, as a rock and as a refuge, and as a hundred other metaphors. God wants to be there for you in the way you need God to be. How do you need God?"

The young man paused for what felt like forever.

"I need God as a Father to give me a long hug," he answered.

In the next few moments he wrapped his arms around himself, pulling his legs into his chest as he began to weep, this time for a long time. He smiled sometimes, and held tighter at others. I checked in with him every so often. He just kept saying, "It feels so good."

When he left that day, I asked him if anything felt different. I'll never forget the profundity of his insight.

"I've been searching after God, and I've been exhausted. But God's been here, right in here the whole time, longing to know me, to hold me, to have me make space for him."

Where Are You?

Hidden in the Garden of Eden, Adam and Eve hear a voice calling for them. I can't imagine how frightened they must have been. The blame game is in full gear by then. Every psychological defense-dynamic named by Sigmund Freud and Carl Jung millennia later is ignited and super-charged.

God says, "Where are you?"

God doesn't say, "What the hell have you done?"

God doesn't say, "Where'd you selfish, ungrateful half-creatures crawl off to?"

No, God expresses curiosity and compassion.

In the spiritual traditions, gods are often angry and impatient. In saying that this is how the God of the Bible responded, I don't at all mean to imply that every page of the Judeo-Christian Scriptures paints a picture of an empathetic, therapist-like God that other religions ought to admire. And I don't mean to proselytize, either. The God of the Christian Scriptures has puzzled many, and numerous scholars have attempted to solve the puzzle.

But these are God's first words. In arranging the many and various narratives of the Bible, it seemed important to those working with these holy texts to give us this small but significant window into God's being. God says, "Where are you?"

But fast-forward to Jesus. Millennia later, we hear God's "Where are you?" in stereo. Father and Son pursue human beings with curiosity and compassion, seeking union amid the many inner divisions that plague us. And the third member of the Trinity, the Spirit, becomes that union, dwelling within us in order to resolve every division, to heal every broken place.

For many years I thought that the God offered to me by Christian pastors was a kind of duplicitous figure, extending grace but with a very big condition. This God would declare me "not guilty" and send me out from his law court "justified," but I'd better not slip up. I'd better not disappoint.

After all, Matthew ends the sections we explored earlier with this stern admonition: "Be perfect as your heavenly father is perfect." Isn't that the end-game for God? Isn't that why we wind up spiritually exhausted despite invitations to grace?

But my perspective on God changed dramatically when I stumbled across Dietrich Bonhoeffer's brief but life-giving words about this text in his *Letters and Papers from Prison.* Citing the original Greek word for "perfect" — *teleios* — along with some original thinking from another scholar, Bonhoeffer affirms a better translation of this text: "Be whole as your heavenly father is whole."[7] And in classic Bonhoeffer form, he says that we'll never get to this wholeness without community.

Whether with a therapist, with a friend, or simply by ourselves with God in prayer, we're drawn into wholeness as we identify and remove every obstacle to union. It's a difficult process. A modern-day therapeutic god would simply tell us to think more positive thoughts, or simply remind us that there is grace for messy people. But the God of the Christian Scriptures goes to great lengths to find us in our hiddenness, to call us out of it through a major Beatitude-inspired surgery, and to invite us to become ambassadors of wholeness for the sake of others.

This invitation to holiness is so very counter-intuitive, a reversal of the exhausting ladder-of-upward-mobility holiness projects offered by exhausted pastors in exhausting churches. It doesn't require superior aptitude, either. It's available to everyone. A. W. Tozer writes, "Holiness, as taught in the Scriptures, is not based upon knowledge on our part. Rather, it is based upon the resurrected Christ in-dwelling us and changing us into His likeness."[8]

God dwelling in us. This is the God who says, "Where are you?" This is Emmanuel — "God with us." This is that slow, patient, lifelong life of holiness that resists the upward-bound forms of super-spirituality which only exhaust.

This holiness I can handle. This holiness isn't exhausting. This holiness is the kind of hard work that leads to wholeness. And I'm up for that. Are you?

If so, let's take the next step toward wholeness.

understanding our *whole* story

In the press of busyness, there is neither time nor quiet to
win the transparency that is indispensable if a man is to
come to understand himself in willing one thing.

SØREN KIERKEGAARD

Who am I? This or the other?
Am I one person today and tomorrow another?

DIETRICH BONHOEFFER

God is more intimate to me than I am to myself.

ST. AUGUSTINE

AS A CHRISTIAN, I'm convinced that every human being is an
image-bearer of God. Our deepest DNA is God-DNA. The
venerable St. Augustine put it bluntly: "God is more intimate to
me than I am to myself."[1] And the fifteenth-century Augustinian
mystic Catherine of Genoa echoes her teacher's thought when she
writes, "My Me is God, nor do I recognize any other Me except
my God Himself."[2]

Our deepest "me" is God. We're one. We're in union. And

sometimes we experience this extraordinary oneness in a moment of communion, or as we're swept into beauty, or connected in a way that feels transcendent.

But then we're jolted back to reality. In a rush, we're welcomed back into our ordinary experience of dividedness. We're aware again of our inner contradictions and frustrated desires. We react out of our reptilian brain, hurting the people we love the most. But perhaps we retain a sense of heart-sickness, a longing which reminds us that division is not our final state.

The division we experience — which, of course, leads to exhaustion and relational turmoil and inner angst — cuts us off from the Deep Well which is God. Unable to draw water from the Life-Giving Fountain, we look near and far for something — anything — that can provide life. An addiction. A drug. A dopamine surge of glory. Cut off from the Inner Light, we look for something — anything — that will illumine the darkness we experience within.

It's as if we've been cut off from the energy source, and thus cut off from our very selves. C. S. Lewis puts it this way:

> And indeed the only way in which I can make real to myself what theology teaches about the heinousness of sin is to remember that every sin is the distortion of an energy breathed into us — an energy which, if not thus distorted, would have blossomed into one of those holy acts whereof "God did it" and "I did it" are both true descriptions.[3]

Lewis intuits the divide as a break in our fundamental oneness and wholeness in God, where our desire and God's desire are the same.

Here's an important point, and one we forget when we're unreflectively going about our busy lives: *Wholeness is our birthright.* Oneness is our most original state of being.

And though our experience of division makes us feel as if we're being pulled in a thousand different directions, we can always —

always — return to our center. Though we may be fractured images of God, we're nonetheless images, restored and matured as we take the time to reflect on our lives, to make sense of our stories, and to experience the oneness for which we've been made.

Losing Oneness

Maybe our best experience of it was in our mother's womb. Perhaps no other space has ever felt so safe. Perhaps at no other point have we felt more "one."

And yet, we know the inevitable outcome. When we're born, we leave the wonderful safety of our mother's womb. We lose the most profound sense of union and connection we can have on earth. From warmth, quiet, and secure rest, we enter into an unimaginably bright, chilly, sterile, and frightening space inhabited by huge people in white uniforms. And we're asked to breathe.

Breathe?

Well, that's a big request! We've never done this before.

And so our very first breath is an anxious one. What we see is a blur. The noise we hear is overwhelming — cries, cheers, many voices talking over each other. Our hearts are racing. Nothing about this feels "normal." Our brains are busy with questions: *Is this OK? Am I OK? And is that my mom? She looks a whole lot different from this angle!*

If we're lucky, we're put on the second-most secure place we'll know in these earliest days — our mother's chest. And if we're placed there just at the time we most need it, our hearts will settle down. We'll feel her warmth. We'll recognize her heartbeat. We'll intuit her love. We'll relax in the reunion. And she will be our first mirror of divine love.

With growing wisdom, we'll quickly learn the skills necessary to make it in this new environment. We'll learn to cry when we're unsettled, insecure, hungry, or afraid. We'll learn to smile in order to mirror Mom's loving gaze (and in the process we'll internalize God's loving gaze). And soon enough, we'll learn to crawl, and even walk, testing our own sense of inner security as we gaze back at our mother's eyes.

But this new environment we've entered isn't always safe.

Soon enough, we'll sense our mother's anxiety and dis-ease. We'll know when our cries are received and when they're met with unexpected resistance. We'll recognize the "No, no, no!" as well as the "Good boy!" We'll hear her yell. We'll feel her fatigue with us. We'll even get passed off to the larger figure with the scratchy beard and odd chest hair, and we'll have to decide whether or not he's safe.

This dynamic of security and insecurity will guide us in our first years. Security and insecurity, in fact, will become a major theme of our young lives — just as they are today.

Taking our cues from Mom, we'll slowly move away from her embrace and into the arms of another, or across the living room floor, or into a Pack n' Play with a friend for some fun.

We might even be brave enough to stay with a babysitter, that sweet fourteen-year-old whose braces glisten and whose laughter makes us smile.

As we grow and change, the dynamic of security and insecurity does too. We're increasingly aware of our mother's moods, of what pleases her and what doesn't. And we hear the fights our parents sometimes have — about money, about love, and sometimes about us.

Born into an imperfect world to imperfect caregivers, no matter how well-intentioned they are, we are subject to a confusing array of messages.

Eat this. Don't eat that.

Play here. Don't play there.

He's good. She's bad.

This is right. That's wrong.

We do our very best, I suspect. As we grow in will and consciousness, we try to do what makes Mommy smile and avoid what makes her frown. But in these early years we are both beautiful and broken little creatures, imperfectly perfect, being both "terrible twos" and terrific twos, innocent and yet a bit devious already.

Now, here's the real dilemma: Whether consciously or not, we intuit that the unacceptable things we do ought to be avoided. Sometimes we intuit that the unacceptable things are closely associated with us, a confusing message for any child. When Mom says, "Good little boys don't get mad," we wonder what to do with our anger.

So what do we do? Poet Robert Bly suggests that from an early age, we put the seemingly unacceptable parts of ourselves into an "invisible bag."[4] So when Mom tells us to stop whining, we consciously or unconsciously put this part of us in the invisible bag, the bag reserved for all the dark, unacceptable parts of us. When Dad yells at us for giggling at the dinner table, we put a bit of our whimsical innocence in the bag. When we wet the bed during a sleepover and a friend says, "Grow up!", we put on our game face, toughen up, and put weakness in the bag. When the pastor says, "Be nice," we put the rebellious part of us in the bag. When our best friend is the fastest runner in grade school, a part of us feels deficient and strives to get faster, and the other part of us that's fine with not being first goes into the bag.

By the time we're in middle school, we're lugging this bag to school along with our backpack, tennis shoes, and trumpet. It gets heavier by the day.

It grows when the guys tell us to stop being a wimp.

It grows when the popular girls tell us that our face is plain and needs more makeup.

It grows in high school when we don't make the cut for the team, and when the school halls are bigger and filled with more students.

It grows as we apply for college, scripting our very best self and putting every not-so-appealing part, including the little incident with the marijuana, into the long, dark, invisible bag.

I suppose the question we continually ask ourselves, in one way or another, is always the same: "What do they want to see, and what should I put away in the bag?"

Our twenties produce much more psychic trash. We pretty ourselves up for the big interview, the blind date, and the first client meeting. During our twenties, psychologists say, we're forming our identity. We're climbing the ladder. We're proving our worth. It's all quite exhausting, but we're young. We'll never be more resilient!

Our work is nearly complete. Our best self has been constructed through a series of conscious and unconscious choices that have divided a once-whole little baby. Of course, a great deal has happened to create this new and complex divided self. But even now, we can't forget our birthright. Even at thirty, with our invisible bag extending ever further behind us, we cannot forget who we are:

> On the one hand, there is the great truth that from the first moment of my existence the deepest dimension of my life is that I am made by God for union with himself. The deepest dimension of my identity as a human person is that I share in God's own life both now and in eternity in a relationship of untold intimacy.
>
> On the other hand, my own daily experience impresses upon me the painful truth that my heart has listened to the serpent instead of to God. There is something in me that puts on fig leaves of concealment, kills my brother, builds towers of confusion, and brings cosmic chaos upon the earth. There is something in me that loves darkness rather than light, that rejects God and thereby rejects my own deepest reality as a human person made in the image and likeness of God.[5]

In a mysterious way, we each bear both the Inner Light of God and the darkness of concealment, an original beauty and innocence as well as a sophisticated radar for danger and a penchant for deceit. We can be a mystery to ourselves. We are known and we are hidden. Even the great St. Paul knew this, exclaiming, "I do not understand my own actions. For I do not do what I want, but I do the very thing I hate" (Rom. 7:15).

As he wrestled with the external realities of good and evil during World War II, theologian and pastor Dietrich Bonhoeffer recognized his own inner battle of darkness and light, asking,

Who am I? This or the other?
Am I one person today and tomorrow another?
Am I both at once? A hypocrite before others,
And before myself a contemptibly woebegone weakling?[6]

Can you relate? Do you find yourself saying, *I don't understand myself?* I hear this all the time from my clients:

I don't understand why I work myself to death.
I don't understand why I'm so drawn to pornography.
I don't understand why I binge and purge.
I don't understand the rage inside of me.
I don't understand . . .

Can we ever understand?

We have opportunities. Sometimes the opportunity comes with age, as we find that we're not as resilient as we once were and we become wearier as we drag the long bag behind us.

Sometimes the opportunity comes when a spouse or a coworker or a friend gets inadvertently hit with the contents of the bag, which, over time, seems to develop holes and seepage.

Sometimes the opportunity comes through significant failure, which requires us to take a long, hard look at who we truly are.

Sometimes the opportunity comes through exhaustion, which leads us into a therapist's office, where we try for the first time to get to know our stories.

My point is that eventually we'll need to open the bag of secrets. Inside, we'll find not just understanding, but the wholeness we seek.

From Division to Wholeness

Thomas Merton once said, "The fall from Paradise was a fall from unity." And perhaps this story of origin held dear by Christians makes the best sense of our own experience, of our own fall from the paradise of perfect union with our mother to the dividedness of our lives as adults. We tell stories, even stories of origin, to make sense of our lives, and I'm a Christian, at least in part, because the Christian story makes the most sense to me.

The earliest Christian theologians, sometimes called "Fathers," told this story too. They told it through icons, through a mysterious meal called Communion, and through times of confession and absolution. Perhaps they intuited our need to be fathered, mothered, held and loved. The liturgy of the church itself became a way of telling the story — daily, weekly, yearly — in order to re-orient, re-story, and re-direct shattered image-bearers.

One of these early Fathers, St. Gregory of Nyssa, is well known for being a pastor to weary pilgrims. In fact, he went on to write books on pastoral care. Gregory knew of the inner division we're exploring here. He believed that human beings were created to image God, but he saw a different reality playing out, a reality named sin among Christians. In fact, these early Fathers viewed sin as a kind of disorientation. It's as if our GPS was scrambled and we were knocked off-course, driving waywardly yet with some remaining intuition of our destination.

For Gregory, humans are both beautiful and broken. He claims that our "godlike beauty" is "hidden under curtains of shame."[7] Perhaps he'd say today that our godlike beauty is hidden in the long, invisible bag. Theologians like Gregory believed that God is more essential to us than we are to ourselves, and that sin represents the veil which prevents us from seeing our greatest beauty. And so, for Gregory, the journey to wholeness — or "virtue," as he calls it — is not about behaving better, but becoming who we truly are.

Frederick Buechner said something similar twenty years ago. He wrote,

> The original, shimmering self gets buried so deep that most of us end up hardly living out of it at all. Instead we live out all the other selves, which we are constantly putting on and taking off like coats and hats against the world's weather.[8]

What Buechner and Gregory see is the kind of dual reality of the divided life. We are both beautiful and broken, emerging and hiding. And because it took us many years to develop our well-honed ability to hide, it takes us a long time to emerge into wholeness, virtue, and beauty.

I sometimes think of the double life of the caterpillar. I'm not a lepidopterist, but I'm told that caterpillars are consuming machines. Their basic instinct is to eat constantly. Left to their own devices, they'd be fat, happy, and crawling along in the dirt their entire lives.

But lying dormant within them are *imaginal* cells. And these cells whisper within, "You were made for something more. You were made to fly!" And so a battle emerges between these growing-and-multiplying imaginal cells and the consuming-caterpillar cells that shout, "Don't listen to that! You were made to crawl in the dirt." But as the imaginal cells continue to proliferate, the caterpillar is transformed in an inevitable process that involves the chrysalis stage, a stage of necessary suffering and change. Yet, while the caterpillar is in the chrysalis, something remarkable happens. The battle ends. As it turns out, the caterpillar's belly-wandering was necessary too. Its life becomes the very source of nutrition for the new life of an emerging butterfly. The transformative process reveals that the two lives are not at cross-purposes but are instead working toward a unity of being, where even the "false self" of the caterpillar is drawn into the beautiful newness to be revealed. As the butterfly finally emerges, it carries with it the life of the caterpillar and the chrysalis, bearing its entire story of brokenness and beauty. Nothing is wasted. Out of death comes life.

The great saint and mystic Meister Eckhart once wrote, "A heart is said to be divided when it is dispersed over many things and towards many ends."[9] Dispersed toward many ends, we exhaust ourselves. We're no more than consuming caterpillars. Unless — unless we listen carefully to the whisper of our imaginal cells. The whisper is an invitation to wholeness that, in the Christian tradition at least, is an invitation to union, oneness with the Three-in-One, who is unity amid multiplicity.

The story of one early Church Father stands out above all as an illustration of this life of competing desires. St. Augustine of Hippo (354-430 C.E.) was a towering figure in early Christianity. His *Confessions* is our earliest instance of theological autobiography. In it he describes a life of lust, sexual meandering, deviousness, greed, and self-promotion — the divided life. He tells his story with remarkable honesty, arguing that the very way to knowing God is through his own memory, through the hard work of knowing himself. With the self-curiosity of a psychologist, he explores a vast internal maze, painting a most elaborate picture of the divided heart:

> What am I then, O my God? What nature am I? A life various and manifold, and exceeding immense. Behold in the plains, and caves, and caverns of my memory, innumerable and innumerably full of innumerable kinds of things, either through images, as all bodies; or by actual presence, as the arts; or by certain notions or impressions, as the affections of the mind, which, even when the mind doth not feel, the memory retaineth.[10]

Somehow Augustine intuits that he will discover God by telling his story, which is tucked away in those vast inner "caves" and "caverns" that represent his long, invisible bag. And he opens that bag and tells his story because he knows what will be revealed:

> Seek for yourself, O man; search for your true self. He who seeks shall find — but, marvel and joy, he will not find himself, he will find God, or, if he find himself, he will find himself in God.[11]

Wholeness, it turns out, is our great inheritance, our deepest and truest self.

The Antidote to Exhaustion: Wholeheartedness

We've spent six chapters diagnosing our soul's dilemma from many different angles. We've explored the findings of researchers and neurobiologists, poets and psychologists. We've revisited my faith tradition, the Christian tradition, through musings on holiness, wholeness, and hiddenness. We're *almost* ready to begin to practice wholeness, to embrace wholeheartedness, which will take courage — and three more chapters.

I'm ending this portion where we started in the Introduction, with the compelling words of the poet David Whyte, whose providential evening with a spiritual sage elicited an extraordinary bit of wisdom that I've now been savoring for more than a decade. You may recall their dialogue over a glass of wine during a time when, after a significant stretch of hard work at a non-profit, Whyte found himself exhausted.

"Tell me about exhaustion," Whyte says.

The old monk responds, "You know that the antidote to exhaustion is not necessarily rest?"

"The antidote to exhaustion is not necessarily rest?" Whyte asks, puzzled, perhaps like you and I might be. "What is it, then?"

His friend answers, "The antidote to exhaustion is wholeheartedness."[12]

The antidote to exhaustion is wholeheartedness?

Wholeheartedness — *wholeness* — is our antidote because to drink of it is to drink from the Original Source, the Life-Giving Fountain, the Three-in-One. Wholeheartedness is a participation in the life of God, of the only whole human being who has ever walked the earth — Jesus. Wholeness dwells in human beings by the Spirit of God, whose divine life pulsates within those who drink at the Well.

It is this birthright that is lost when we get in the way, as the tale of Adam and Eve vividly reminds us. Merton writes,

> After Adam had passed through the centre of himself and emerged on the other side to escape from God by putting himself between himself and God, he had mentally reconstructed the whole universe in his own image and likeness. That is the painful and useless labor which has been inherited by his descendants — the labor of science without wisdom, the mental toil that pieces together fragments that never manage to coalesce in one completely integrated whole; the labor of action without contem-

plation that never ends in peace or satisfaction, since no task is finished without opening the way to ten more tasks that have to be done.[13]

When we live apart from this promised wholeness, we effectively participate in that "original" sin which, in one sense, is an exhausting striving to be more than we are. It is a refusal to accept our *perfectly* limited humanity, with bodies and minds and hearts that crave the *shalom* offered. As Merton points out, the result is painful labor, mental toil, and an inability to piece together our fragmented lives. Clearly, the only antidote to this dire state is wholeness.

If we take Bly's advice, we will open that long, invisible bag. We'll take a close look at its contents and at our lives. We'll open ourselves to "becoming" who we are as we remove the curtains of shame. As we change, our praying will change too, as we'll see in the next section. Another favorite monk of mine, James Finley, writes, "We pray not to recharge our batteries for the business of getting back to the concerns of daily life, but rather to be transformed by God so that the myths and fictions of our life might fall like broken shackles from our wrists."[14]

As we will discover, our deepest prayer is a prayer for participation in God's life of wholeness. It is a searching out of our guarded and hidden hearts, exposing the myths and fictions that keep us divided. We cannot do this alone. We were not made to do this alone. *Alone* has left us exhausted. *Alone* has left us leading lives of quiet desperation. *Alone* enslaves us to a sinister foe — the false self. *Alone* renders us incapable of love and generosity.

But as we will find out, solitude is different from aloneness. In solitude, we can cultivate wholeness. In solitude, we fall in love — or, better said, into Love. Our restored hearts can love wholeheartedly, as they were created to love, because love defines a life of flourishing, of *shalom*.

In and with God, we cannot help but live the life of God, who is defined as Love in the First Epistle of John. Once again, the venerable St. Augustine points the way to a life of wholeness that renews our hearts and enables us to love God and neighbor wholeheartedly:

> Once for all, then, a short precept is given you:
> Love, and do what you will:
> whether you hold your peace,
> through love hold your peace;
> whether you cry out, through love cry out;
> whether you correct, through love correct;
> whether you spare, through love do you spare:
> let the root of love be within,
> of this root can nothing spring but what is good.[15]

What I have found, both in my own life and among others, is that we haven't been trained in solitude, in wholeness, in love. We find churches to be places of guilt and shame rather than schools of life-giving wholeness. We find workplaces rewarding the hardest-working rather than the most whole. We define success by what we've achieved — not by how we do what we do — and so are crushed in the face of failure.

In our exhaustion, we medicate, we modify with cosmetic tweaks, we inhale and imbibe. We run from reality rather than toward Reality. We abandon wholeness in our self-help fascinations and machinations. We sabotage maturity through our guilt-and-shame tactics. But it's time to change these life-quenching patterns.

The final three chapters are an invitation to your life, which is Life itself. This isn't an invitation to an idea, but an invitation to an experience known only through participation. There is no quick fix or fast track to wholeness, no surefire method for experiencing perpetual heights of intimacy with God — only the invitation to dwell deeply in God's life, which already dwells in you. As mystics and contemplatives have said for centuries, this journey is not so much about *feeling* as it is about *being*.

When your very *being* experiences transformation, the change that happens may not even be perceptible at first. But with the vision and practice we'll explore, we'll be tapping into a deeper and more transformative experience, where neural patterns shift from reactivity to reflection, where the brain functions as a whole, where our invisible bags hold no weight, where head meets heart, where division melts into wholeness.

So, may the *shalom* of God, which surpasses all understanding, guard your hearts and your minds in Christ Jesus (Phil. 4:7).

Part 3

EXPERIENCING WHOLENESS

IN THESE FINAL CHAPTERS, I invite you to continue your own journey into wholeness more fully and to engage your life more intentionally. As you're reading these chapters, you'll notice that I've included text boxes that offer an array of questions, quotations, and observations that serve as prompts for further reflection. I encourage you to read and reflect on these pages at a slower pace. I would also encourage you to read them with a trusted friend or significant other.

returning to our core, recovering our true self

You do not have to be good.
You do not have to walk on your knees
for a hundred miles through the desert, repenting.
You only have to let the soft animal of your body
     love what it loves.
Tell me about despair, yours, and I will tell you mine.
Meanwhile the world goes on.
Meanwhile the sun and the clear pebbles of the rain
are moving across the landscapes,
over the prairies and the deep trees,
the mountains and the rivers.
Meanwhile the wild geese, high in the clean blue air,
are heading home again.
Whoever you are, no matter how lonely,
the world offers itself to your imagination,
calls to you like the wild geese, harsh and exciting —
over and over announcing your place
in the family of things.[1]

MARY OLIVER

You're not here to find a quick fix. You've embarked on a journey.

Perhaps you picked up this book because you long for something more, a deeper and more centered life. I want to commend you for that. To live from our deep center is to live fully and freely, and to flourish.

But let's be honest. Some days you find yourself exhausted, burning every last ounce of gas in your tank. But you press on because you feel you have to. Navigating quickly through the fast-food drive-through, you sustain yourself with fat and sugar, then rub your aching belly as your mix of heartburn, anxiety, and self-loathing form a toxic cocktail that slowly erodes your capacity for real rest.

Some days you re-commit to disciplining yourself. A critical voice inside says, "Get it together!" And one of the things you re-commit to is a holiness strategy that helps appease the guilt, but doesn't satisfy the deeper longing.

Because you've read this far, however, I want to challenge you to go deeper, to go further. In this chapter I'll invite you to engage in a way that acknowledges your deepest core, your truest self, the most important key to a future of wholeness. (This engagement will allow you to move on to the next chapter, where we'll work more intentionally with the various parts of you that feel the exhausting pull to and fro.)

Mary Oliver invites you to experience this true self in these very provocative words:

You do not have to be good.
You do not have to walk on your knees
for a hundred miles through the desert, repenting.
You only have to let the soft animal of your body
    love what it loves.

> What do you think of Oliver's poetic invitation? Are you
> willing to accept it? Are you ready to accept it? What feelings
> does it stir up inside you?

I remember the first time I heard this poem. My inner Doctrinal Policeman whispered, "That's heresy!" But at my core, I
felt a kind of holy permission to let go of my anxious striving for
perfection and to trust a deeper current flowing within.

What if God was giving you permission to live the only life
you've been given — your own? What if that meant sacrificing
every other life you're trying to live? This would take extraordinary
courage. It would mean trusting that your deepest you is, in fact,
God within you. It would mean leaning into your deepest Desire
— which, in fact, is God-breathed desire. It would mean surrender
— letting "the soft animal of your body love what it loves."

This is what I'm inviting you to.

Getting Acquainted with Our Inner Terrain

I want to suggest something that wise spiritual souls have embraced
for thousands of years, yet something that those of us groomed in
the materialistic West might struggle with. Here it is:

> Your deepest longing is not a longing for a good marriage, or for the se-
> curity of a well-paying job, or even for the end to chronic pain. These are
> all valid and significant longings. But they are only echoes of the lasting
> satisfaction for which you've been created.

The journey from division to wholeness is one in which we
relax our tightly controlled grip on our *little-d* desires, realizing

that they are not our true satisfaction but echoes and foretastes of our ultimate Desire.

> The first thing that you have to do, before you even start thinking about such a thing as contemplation, is to try to recover your basic natural unity, to reintegrate your compartmentalized being into a coordinated and simple whole and learn to live as a unified human person.
>
> Thomas Merton

Most of the time, we barely have a hint of this Desire. We're so busy and preoccupied that we're tuned in to different rhythms — rhythms that actually deplete Desire and foster resignation, exhaustion, and despair. We're left with little time to ask, "Is this where I want to be?" The question itself feels selfish. But the fact is that we'll never have whole selves to offer the world unless we ask it.

Jesus asks the question frequently: "What do you want?" This is a *big-W* Want. But to begin to intuit this, we must often die to our little wants. The spiritual traditions call this process *detachment*. And it begins by recognizing what we've attached our desires to. For most of us, there are a hundred things we could name, from ice cream to our most intimate relationships, from favorite films to financial success. We need not abandon the intimate relationship or stop eating ice cream. But we must see how we've attached our hopes too tightly to these smaller wants. We must see how every attachment is an obstacle to re-connection with our True Self.

We begin by paying attention to our hearts. Every heart is the center, the wellspring of life (Prov. 4:23). We often live disconnected from our hearts, reacting anxiously to whatever demands our urgent attention. But we yearn for freedom, the freedom to live and love with our whole heart, life, and strength.

> There are some men and women who have lived forty or fifty years in the world and have had scarcely one hour's discourse with their hearts all the while.
>
> John Flavel, seventeenth-century
> Presbyterian clergyman

So let me help you move toward that freedom.

Begin now by taking a *very* deep breath and exhaling slowly. Breathe in. Breathe out.

How was it?

It might have made you skeptical: *Isn't every fitness guru today telling us how to breathe?* But this intentional calming and restoring of the breath has been used by many spiritual teachers over the centuries.

It might also have made you realize that you haven't breathed much lately — not fully. And that deep, regular breathing is important — a significant part of the contemplative life, a descending back into our own bodies, a surrendering of our anxious preoccupations for just a few moments in order to find our center. Deep, regular breathing is a sign that we're living mindfully, intentionally, wholly.

After I take a few deep breaths, I like to listen for that question God asked Adam and Eve so long ago: "Where are you?" Do you recall that question from the third chapter of Genesis? Hiding behind hastily made fig-leaf cloaks, humanity's first parents cowered in fear. But as the story goes, God pursued them, looking longingly for his lost children.

As I breathe, I ask myself, "Where are you, Chuck?" And I

listen carefully to my inner being for the responses, welcoming every one.

When you do this, you may hear a variety of responses:

I don't have time for this.
I'm buried under a mound of to-do's.
I'm too ashamed to come out of hiding.
I'm worried about next week's big presentation.
I'm terrified about what will happen in my marriage.
I'm suspicious of this exercise.
I'm just trying to figure out how I can get home in time for my son's concert.
I'm trying to be here, to be present.
I'm itching for a drink.
I'm trying desperately not to fail.

It's hard to listen to all these different voices, but you must. You must welcome every scattered voice from the vast realms of your soul. This takes a bit of time, and sometimes a pen and a journal. It's important to listen, and listen well.

This inner listening is the first step toward discovering your True Self. Your True Self is the "I" that is listening within. It has various names in various traditions — St. Paul calls it the "new self," while some Eastern traditions call it the "old self," because of its primal role beneath every other voice. The early Christian tradition called it the Godself, while more recent spiritual sages have called it the "True Self" or the "Inner Light." Thomas Kelly, the early twentieth-century Quaker missionary and mystic, calls it the "Divine Center":

Deep within us all, there is an amazing inner sanctuary of the soul, a holy place, a Divine Center, a speaking Voice, to which we may continuously return. Eternity is at our hearts, pressing upon our time-torn lives, warming us with intimations of an astounding destiny, calling us home unto itself.[2]

This True Self is made to experience extraordinary union and communion with God. It is our spiritual center, the dwelling place of the Spirit. If we could live from this center and core, we'd live with the kind of patience, kindness, gentleness, and self-control that St. Paul calls "fruits of the Spirit."

But as we listen within, we notice other scattered voices — vying for attention, arguing with us, hiding from us, and sometimes sabotaging us. We must pay attention to these inner strangers, because they'll tell us something of our lost story, revealing longings long forgotten.

Each voice is an indicator revealing one of our heart's attachments. Each gives us a window into a place where Desire's energy is being depleted. Each helps us honestly respond to God's "Where are you?" In fact, as we listen to and welcome each voice, we might even imagine the Spirit within listening compassionately and attentively, eager for the wholeness we long for.

> Within the heart are unfathomable depths. There are reception rooms and bedchambers in it, doors and porches, and many offices and passages. In it is the workshop of righteousness and of wickedness. In it is death; in it is life. . . . The heart is Christ's palace: there Christ the King comes to take his rest, with the angels and spirits of the saints, and he dwells there, walking within it and placing his Kingdom there. . . . The heart is but a small vessel: and yet dragons and lions are there, and there are poisonous creatures and all the treasures of wickedness; rough, uneven places are

> there, and gaping chasms. There likewise is God, there are the angels, there life and the Kingdom, there light and the apostles, the heavenly cities and the treasures of grace. All things are there.
>
> St. Macarius, fourth-century Egyptian monk

If you haven't done much of this kind of work, you might find yourself overwhelmed at this point. Twenty different internal voices might be swirling within you right now. You might feel the inner division in a palpable way. Or you might wonder if you're just a little crazy. No, you're not — you're just not accustomed to disrupting your fragmented inner ecosystem, an ecosystem that's a bit frazzled right now. This is why you must go slowly, carefully. This is work done in weeks, months, and years, not in minutes.

You may want to give yourself a few minutes away from your inner reflection. Fix a cup of tea in the meantime, or take a bath. It's good to take care of your body as you do this work. But when you're ready, return to it.

The Contemplative Descent

There is an extraordinary picture of the absolute loneliness and despair of our exhausting, addictive lives tucked away in the book of Isaiah. In it, a picture is painted of someone who desperately tries to control his life, working every angle and exhausting every opportunity, trying to evade God's "Where are you?" until he is exposed and alone,

> like a flagstaff on the top of a mountain,
> like a signal on a hill. (Isa. 30:17)

Sometimes our anxious striving drives us up the metaphorical mountain. We climb the ladder of success. Perhaps we climb over the backs of friends and colleagues to get to the top. But when we get there, we find ourselves alone. Along the way we've gathered what we thought might bring security, success, or serenity — only to find that they've brought sickness, sadness, and shame. It's lonely at the top.

> And so with his great grace
> he kindled your desire,
> and fastened it to a leash of longing.
>
> Anonymous, *The Cloud of Unknowing*

But God's response is not to mock or condemn. The response to the one left alone on the mountaintop in the book of Isaiah is heartening: "The LORD waits to be gracious to you" (Isa. 30:18). God's "Where are you?" is relentless — but gracious.

God is infinitely patient with us — far more patient than we are with ourselves. Don't take my word for it. John Calvin, the great sixteenth-century pastor and theologian, says it much better. Forgive the length of this quote, but drink it in deeply:

> I insist not so strictly on evangelical perfection, as to refuse to acknowledge as a Christian any man who has not attained it. In this way all would be excluded from the Church, since there is no man who is not far removed from this perfection, while many, who have made but little progress, would be undeservedly rejected.
>
> What then? Let us set this before our eye as the end at which we ought constantly to aim. Let it be regarded as the goal towards which we are to run. For you cannot divide the matter with God, undertaking part of what his word enjoins, and omitting part at pleasure. For, in the first

place, God uniformly recommends integrity as the principal part of his worship, meaning by integrity real singleness of mind, devoid of gloss and fiction, and to this is opposed a double mind; as if it had been said, that the spiritual commencement of a good life is when the internal affections are sincerely devoted to God, in the cultivation of holiness and justice.

But seeing that, in this earthly prison of the body, no man is supplied with strength sufficient to hasten in his course with due alacrity, while the greater number are so oppressed with weakness, that hesitating, and halting, and even crawling on the ground, they make little progress, let every one of us go as far as his humble ability enables him, and prosecute the journey once begun. No one will travel so badly as not daily to make some degree of progress.[3]

We crawl along, always reaching, making less progress than we'd like. But this is the journey — from that lonely, exposed place where we find ourselves after clawing our way to the top, to the lush valley below with streams of living water. The journey is from a place of exhaustion to a place of rest, from a place of fragmentation to a place of wholeness and wholeheartedness.

I call this journey the *contemplative descent*. In contrast to the upward mobility of our world, this is the way of downward mobility. And I see it as a descent into wholeness.

> Now you have to stand in desire,
> all your life long,
> if you are to make progress in the way of wholeness.
> This desire must always be at work in your will,
> by the power of almighty God
> and by your own consent.
>
> Anonymous, *The Cloud of Unknowing*

This descent can happen to us without our consent. We might fail at a significant relationship. Or find ourselves wrestling with a life-threatening illness. Or experience a series of humiliations that knock us off our mountaintop.

But sometimes God kindles within us a desire for something more — more life, more intimacy, more freedom. If we are attentive to God's whisper, Desire will lead us where we must go. And the way we must go is downward, as Jesus went downward. Jesus once said,

> Come to me, all you that are weary and are carrying heavy burdens, and I will give you rest. Take my yoke upon you, and learn from me; for I am gentle and humble in heart, and you will find rest for your souls. For my yoke is easy, and my burden is light. (Matt. 11:28-30)

We become more whole as we unburden ourselves, *as we let go of what we thought we needed in order to experience what we already have.*

Now, imagine that you've made the difficult climb to the top of your mountain. It's the place you thought was your destination, but it's the place where you find yourself alone, exhausted, and seemingly out of resources. It's the place where some other part of you beyond your True Self took you in its attempt to save your life, but the mountaintop is now a place of great peril.

Imagine yourself here, surrounded by the baggage you've carried on your back. What does it look like? What does it feel like? How have you held up?

Do you want to descend? Do you want to relinquish the back-breaking effort to get your *little-d* desires fulfilled on your own terms? Are you willing to admit that you can't manage your own happiness? Are you longing for rest, once and for all?

Letting Go

In this imaginative exercise, it's important for each of us to survey the land, to see what we've been clinging to, what we're burdened by, what we've climbed so far to attain. But it's not helpful to demonize what we find.

Many of the things we've carried with us are valuable — relationships, work, service to others, academic success, financial security, religious knowledge. The problem, as I've noted before, is that we've given each of these far too much weight. They've become too prominent, too meaningful, too central to our identity. They've come to demand too much of our energy. And we're being pulled to and fro as we attempt to maintain each one.

Jesus, who tended to speak in hyperbole, makes it clear that even the best things in life can become burdens, including those whom we love the most:

> Whoever comes to me and does not hate father and mother, wife and children, brothers and sisters, yes, and even life itself, cannot be my disciple. Whoever does not carry the cross and follow me cannot be my disciple. (Luke 14:26-27)

This sounds strange to our modern ears, but Jesus is telling us how to descend the mountain. Of course, because he speaks through great exaggeration, we need to recognize that he isn't asking us to hate our family. He's saying to us, "You must let go. You must find your identity in me, not in anything or anyone else." For those of us who've found it difficult to "cut the cord," this is a great piece of psychological wisdom from Jesus.

As we name what demands our attention and commands our allegiance, we must also take the time to consider how these people and things might continue to accompany us without unduly burdening us.

The contemplative life doesn't demand that we abandon everything we've loved or attained. We need not become ascetic or sell every possession. But we must learn the posture of the ascetic and be ready to be without. In fact, what we relinquish is the need to possess. Our desire, which has become addicted to possession, must learn dispossession. This is the only way that our *big-D* Desire can be freed.

Mary Oliver gives us a hint at what this letting go and dispossession require:

> You only have to let the soft animal of your body
>> love what it loves.

But her use of "only." Doesn't that word sound strange? Or perhaps naïve?

Letting go isn't easy, and I suspect that Oliver would agree. Surrendering the weighty burdens of our *little-d* desires isn't a simple matter.

This *only* of Oliver's may take three hours, three days, or three years. This *only* may take forty years in the desert. This *only* may require unwanted suffering. This *only* may require many dyings and risings.[4]

It takes this long because we're so attached to our baggage. It's difficult to let go of what has come to mean so much. It's difficult to wake up to the possible newness of life when we've become so accustomed to the old. We may find that we have to deal with each burden we've carried up the mountain on its own. We won't experience freedom overnight. And if we're addicted to the quick fix, this will be very hard for us to hear.

We're at a crossroads in life.

The point I'm trying to make is that letting go isn't a behavior. It's not another to-do. It's an *entering-in* to a new way of life by way of daily surrender, dispossession, and even humiliation.

As we let go, we may begin to feel the effects. Just as an addict goes through withdrawal when giving up a drug, so our surrender will produce emotional and physical symptoms. We may feel even more tired, sometimes nauseous, often sad, and almost always anxious. (At this point, you're probably thinking, "What a helpful book this is!") Surrender is hard.

> Have you ever experienced withdrawal symptoms in any way? As you survey the things/relationships/emotions/practices you find yourself attached to, what will be hardest to let go of?

As I've entered into my own journey of descent in fits and starts, I've often felt as if I wasn't doing enough. As someone who's addicted to busyness, I've experienced a range of feelings when I've surrendered it — I've felt ashamed, unimportant, useless, anxious about how others are viewing me, empty, even lonely. Without my familiar "friends" of activity, I've felt somewhat lost. And it's been extremely difficult to "sit" with these feelings. It would have been much easier to find something to do — a book to read (or write!), a lecture to prepare, a person to help.

Although we're invited to descend, the reality is that many of us don't. Some of us can't. Some of us don't know how to do it. Most of us don't have spiritual directors or wise mentors who've navigated this journey themselves. Once again, we're often left with simplistic spiritual recipes instead of an honest vision of mature descent. In this void, God often takes over by using our life's circumstance — and our sufferings in particular — to get our attention.

Spiritual sages of old tell us that these are the times in which a cloud can descend on our mountaintop, ushering in a "dark night of the soul." These times are providential roadblocks on the frantic highways of our lives. St. John writes,

> As God sets the soul in this dark night, He allows it not to find attraction or sweetness in anything whatsoever. If those souls to whom this comes to pass knew how to be quiet at this time, then they would delicately experience this inward refreshment in that ease and freedom from care. In this state of contemplation, it is God Who is now working in the soul. He binds its interior faculties, and allows it not to cling to the understanding, nor to have delight in the will, nor to reason with the memory. God communicates by pure spirit. From this time forward, imagination and fancy can find no support in any meditation. Spiritual persons suffer great trials from the fear of being lost on the road and that God has abandoned them. Let them trust in God, who will bring them into the clear and pure light of love.[5]

During this dark night, we're no longer satisfied by the high of our addictive pace of life, or the solace of our spiritual quick fixes, or the consolation from a close friend. We're frustrated in our praying. Our therapy seems to produce no results. Our typical standbys — wine, chocolate, sports, even naps — do not fulfill. As St. John says, we do not experience the typical sweetness or attraction of our old addictions. But at the same time, we're not experienced in sitting quietly with these frustrations. But St. John offers a surprising consolation: God has not abandoned us, but is actually at work deep within us, wrestling our desires away from the things that have enslaved them.

Have you had a "dark night of the soul"? How did you experience it? Did you sense God at work in it?

Can we trust the process? This may be the hardest thing required of us. It's often difficult for us to do when we feel as if we can manage our lives, at least in some ways. But this is our invitation. We need to trust sages and poets like Mary Oliver, who remind us that we only have to let the soft animal of our body love what it loves. We need to trust saints and sages like St. John of the Cross, who believe that the God-implanted *big-D* Desire is more essential to us than the scattered half-desires that rule our hearts. The anonymous author of *The Cloud of Unknowing* echoes this, saying,

> Let that meek [quiet] darkness be your whole mind and like a mirror to you. For I want your thought of self to be as naked and simple as your thought of God, so that you may be with God in spirit without fragmentation and scattering of your mind.[6]

In other words, we're asked to let go, to surrender, to trust the process, to trust that the deepest desire of our heart is God-desire. And in trusting, we are honoring something deeper within us, our deepest selves, where God dwells. Or, as the great mystics might say, we're trusting that God in us will love what God loves.

From Many to One

I began this book by describing the experience of our busy lives as being pulled in a thousand different directions. What we're learning is that the wisdom of spiritual writers from centuries ago is connecting closely with a prevailing psychological wisdom available to us today.

In the next chapter I'm going to introduce my own synthesis of the insights from both spiritual wisdom and psychological wisdom, and then offer a way for us to work mindfully and intentionally with the various parts of ourselves that seem to be pulled to and fro.[7] But we couldn't start this process without first acknowledging the reality of our deep, True Self, which is "hidden with Christ in God" (Col. 3:3).

We cannot begin to live wholly unless we're connected to our True Self, which is our Whole Self. If we're busily addicted on our mountaintops of success and striving, we'll lack the contemplative presence necessary to gaze within. And if we're looking for something to help us feel a little better right this minute, we'll be bitterly disappointed.

No one needs to be a mystic to proceed — not me, not you. You need only to have the desire to live from your deepest core. When you acknowledge that desire, you're greeting God within you, who longs more deeply than you ever will for union, intimacy, and oneness of heart. You are speaking the words of St. Augustine: God is "more intimate to me than I am to myself."[8]

This may mean that you slow down at this point, returning to the beginning of this chapter and proceeding through it more slowly and meditatively. It may mean that you wrestle for some time with Mary Oliver's words, listening within with wonder for desiring "the soft animal of your body" to be pulsing with life and hope. It may mean that you connect with a friend on this journey. But remember: you are at a crossroads, and this journey is not and will not be easy.

Over the course of many years you've become exhausted and divided. Your many "selves" have stories to tell — stories we'll explore in the next chapter. Give yourself the grace to take this journey as slowly and deliberately as you can, knowing that God is committed to doing the most significant work from the inside out.

Below I provide two exercises that will help you slow down, pay attention, and become more aware of what's happening within. Don't ignore these or try to hurry through them. If you undertake them mindfully, they'll help you cultivate an inner sense of presence and awareness, which is critical for the next stage.

Know that God is infinitely more patient with you than you are with yourself. As you commit to this slow process, you will find that your shame will dissolve before God's smiling face, your heart will rest, and you'll feel the surge of loving energy that comes from deep within and is enough to sustain you through the rest of your journey.

Exercise 1

Get in a comfortable, upright posture in a chair and spend ten minutes in silence. To begin, take deep breaths in and out. Relax. Just be open to what you feel, see, and hear. Try not to judge what you're doing or how you're doing it. Simply pay attention, receiving and welcoming whatever stirs, whatever comes to you.

When you're done, write down or process with a friend what you experienced. Did you notice "voices" in your mind making a wide range of comments? Did you notice your mind wandering? If so, the "You" that noticed these things is the most important discovery of all. It is your True Self, your Center, your Inner Light. We often live disconnected from our True Self, simply reacting rather than reflecting.

In the coming days, repeat this exercise. Simply relax your breathing and pay attention. Write down what you see, feel, hear — words, images, bodily sensations. Try to increase the amount of time you spend in this silence.

Exercise 2

Sitting comfortably in a chair, enter into silence again. As you deepen your breathing and relax, focus on your body. Notice your back against the chair, your feet on the floor, the shirt on your back, your hands and feet, your neck and upper back. Continue on, noticing every part of your body — from temples to toes. Again, simply pay attention. Notice what you feel. You'll probably start to feel increasingly relaxed, perhaps even sleepy. This is perfectly fine.

In the coming days, repeat this exercise whenever you can. Simply cultivate your inner sense of presence and awareness.

These exercises will help you cultivate a deeper connection with your True Self, and will give you a taste of rest and wholeness on their own.[9]

CHAPTER 8

cultivating wholeness amid our scattered selves

Purity of heart is to will one thing.

Søren Kierkegaard

As soon as I start a dialogue with myself, the reality of the self as a kind of society becomes apparent at once. The sense of inner dividedness can be bitter.

Martin Smith

The very contradictions in my life are in some ways God's mercy to me.

Thomas Merton

IN THE PREVIOUS CHAPTER we took some time to cultivate inner awareness, recognizing that in our frazzled lives we're often disconnected from our deepest core, our True Self. I encouraged you to spend time in silence, to become acquainted with the many diverse voices and images in your inner world.

Perhaps you've imagined yourself on the mountaintop I described in Chapter 7, exhausted from carrying the baggage of your life. Maybe you've got a mental picture of that baggage strewn everywhere, and you're asking yourself, "Where do I go from here?"

It can be disconcerting to do the work of wholeness. Control freaks that we are, most of us try to maintain our organized chaos. But as we become more aware of our inner life, it can be disruptive to realize that there are voices within which are in conflict.

As we discovered in Chapter 3, it's true that we all experience a kind of inner multiplicity in life. Just the other day, my younger daughter was feeling anxious about a decision she needed to make: watch a movie with Dad, or hang out with her friend. "A part of me really wants to hang with my friend," she told me, "but you and I don't get to do the movie thing very often!" We played with this idea a bit. Jokingly, I pulled one of her arms and asked, "What does this side of you say?" Then I pulled the other arm and asked, "What about this one?" We both laughed. And then I pointed at her heart and said, "What does Maggie want to do?" After a few minutes, she knew what she wanted: "I think I'd like to spend a few hours with my friend first, and then tell her I'd like to spend the rest of the night with you." I smiled. "Sounds like a good decision, Maggie."

Episcopal priest Martin Smith explains this kind of inner conflict:

As soon as I start a dialogue with myself, the reality of the self as a kind of society becomes apparent at once. I ask myself a question. So there are two selves for a start, one asking and one being asked! It takes two to have a dialogue. We continually address ourselves, our selves. When we encourage ourselves, there is a courageous self and a timid self in conversation. When we blame ourselves, there is a moral self accusing a self who failed. Sometimes these other selves belong to the past. Memories of past behavior can fill us with pride or loathing, and we congratulate or abominate the self we once were and that lives on within us. Or we find ourselves feeling and acting in ways that stem from experiences of long ago but are out of keeping with the present situation. It is as if the selves we once were linger on within and have power to seize the reins from time to time. I experience more selves when I become aware of inner conflict around decisions. One voice beckons me in one direction, then another speaks in contradiction, luring me in another. The sense of inner dividedness can be bitter.[1]

While inner dividedness can be disconcerting, we must acknowledge it. We will move forward in our journey only if we recognize the importance of each and every voice within. While each one can hijack wholeness, I believe that, taken together, these voices hold the hidden treasures of our life.

I've found a particular metaphor to be especially helpful in this kind of work. Imagine your True Self as the Inner Conductor of a large internal orchestra. Perhaps you've been to see the Chicago Symphony or the New York Philharmonic, with their vast array of violins and violas, timpani and trumpets, bassoons and trombones, all working in concert at the direction of the conductor. We appreciate the beauty of this experience because every part works in *symphony,* in harmony, as if each separate will was brought into accord with the will of the conductor. Those of us who've played in bands and orchestras know how much work it takes to achieve this symphonic excellence — careful watching and listening, an awareness of the other musicians, an understanding of when it's our time to shine and when it's our time to rest.

Our inner world works on a similar principle. It's a delicate ecosystem that actually tends toward wholeness, a surprising realization for many who find themselves fragmented and frazzled. According to neurobiologist Daniel Siegel, "There is a natural drive for complex systems to move toward integration, toward wholeness, toward health."[2] And yet, life's difficulties bring about dis-ease and dis-integration. As a consequence, wholeness is disrupted, particularly as a result of early life traumas, which disable critical neural connections and form disordered neural patterns. Siegel explains:

> Various mind states can be defensively created to attempt to avoid reminders of what may have been a potentially painful and confusing way in which the "self" was obliterated in these various settings in the past. Parental intrusions or unavailability in insecure attachment, a history of being bullied at school by peers, or feeling a lack of place and identity within a bustling and anonymous culture can each be the soil from which inner turmoil grows. In these situations, the "self" is not clearly formed as both a differentiated entity and, at the same time, an entity linked intimately with supportive others. Extreme forms of impairments to integration [cause] the self [to] take refuge in excessive withdrawal and differentiation or to become lost in intense anxiety-driven longings for connection.[3]

Siegel, among others in the fields of attachment psychology and interpersonal neurobiology, reminds us that the kinds of "mind states" we experience are learned in our relational matrix, and likewise can be healed in a healthy relational matrix. That gives us hope, especially when it feels like our frazzled, fragmented state is the *final* state.

I see three critical factors involved in this healing work of wholeness and integration — awareness, story, and relationship. Let's explore their connection.

Awareness, Story, and Relationship

This "trinity" of wholeness is something you've already started to practice and experience, beginning with the exercises in the previous chapter. Perhaps it's something you've been working on in and through therapy, spiritual direction, or pastoral care, or even in the rhythms of journaling, art, or daily prayer. There's a multitude of ways to cultivate these three vital aspects of wholeness.

Let's begin with *awareness*. In the previous chapter, you cultivated a deeper awareness of your inner life. You became aware, I hope, of your inner experience and a still deeper Desire beneath the many smaller desires of your life. You became more *mindful,* bringing your intentional attention to your emotions, your body, and the images and words that arose within you. This kind of awareness is crucial, because too often in our busyness we forfeit it to the tyranny of the urgent.

This inner awareness has the potential to cultivate curiosity within. Your inner "I" sees the orchestra playing out of sync and asks, "What's happening here?" When you trace the signals that arise from within by way of emotions, body cues, images, or words, you can bring your curiosity into dialogue with the various parts of you to which you've awakened.

For example, many of us hear an "Inner Critic," a part of us that seems to regularly critique what we do, how we look, and what we say. You can bring your curiosity and attention to this part of you and wonder about its *story* — what might it want to say, to show you, to disclose about your inner world? Simple inner conversations can reveal aspects of your larger story. And what's remarkable, according to Curt Thompson, is that "the process of reflecting on and telling others your story, and the way you experience others hearing it, actually shapes the story and the very neural correlates, or networks, it represents."[4]

> Take a moment to be silent, take a deep breath, and pay attention to a voice within that may be critical of you right now.

What is this "Inner Critic" saying? How does it shame you, berate you, question you, even discourage you from pursuing your own wholeness? How might you engage it and change this conversation?

Another part of you that you might become aware of may feel quite young. Some time ago in my own therapy, I remember having the sense that a very young part of me was scared. It took time to tune into this sensation, but eventually I felt his presence. I became aware of an image of this small child hiding under a side table next to a couch in the living room of the home I grew up in. In fact, I could get a sense of just how young he was simply by remembering the arrangement of the furniture. This scared little boy seemed to hold a lot of anxiety. From his vantage point, the world was a scary place.

I've spent much time listening to what this very young part of me has to say because, in truth, I'm still that scared little boy sometimes. In fact, I believe that we all hold parts of us that feel very young, parts of us that feel very scared, and parts of us that may even feel locked into a particular time and place where we experienced trauma. Each of us has a story, and each of us has learned to cope in different ways with the broken world in which we live.

Can you identify with this story? Do you experience a part of you that feels young? If so, simply listen within, writing down what you sense you are feeling, seeing, and hearing.

As you and all of us on the journey cultivate awareness and become acquainted with our stories, we recognize that both our wounding and our wholeness exist within the matrix of *relationship*. Our stories reveal significant relational characters — our mothers and fathers, a person who bullied or abused us, a teacher who showed us love, a neighbor who pestered us, a God who wanted more for us. And what psychologists and neurobiologists tell us is that in our adult life, we seem to find our way into similar relational patterns. We marry a spouse like our parent; when another person threatens us, we react in fear as we did when we were bullied; we crave attention just as we did with our first-grade teacher. We realize that our so-called issues are often quite old, even as parts of us that we become aware of are revealed as quite young. People are often surprised to feel like their six-year-old self in particular mind-states, or like they're in middle school again in others.

In becoming aware and telling our stories in the context of redemptive relationships, we experience a longed-for sense of wholeness, integration, and overall health in our living and relating. In other words, relationship matters. What we know from science and Scripture is that we are both wounded in relationship and healed in it. Our divided hearts cannot heal in a vacuum. At some level, the healing journey requires relational vulnerability — slowly but surely letting others in, slowly but surely letting God in. It takes tremendous courage to tell our stories and let others in, let alone God. But it is a way of showing ourselves compassion, of being kind to ourselves so that bit by bit we can be gathered back into wholeness.

What psychologists and neurobiologists as well as the great spiritual writers recognize is that compassion for the many conflicted parts of ourselves is critical to growth, maturation, and wholeness. And God's compassionate stance toward us can be a huge source of encouragement. Martin Smith writes,

> The Holy Spirit of God dwells in your heart and is no stranger to the diversity and conflict there. The Spirit dwells with and among and be-

tween all the selves of your self. There is no secret place where the Spirit has no access, nor any inner person excluded from the Spirit's presence.[5]

Indeed, the True Self, participating in the life of the Spirit, is the conduit of love and compassion to every diverse and dis-eased part of us. Let's explore how this participation is possible in a way that is eminently practical.

The Way of Self-Compassion

Back in the mid-2000s, my clinical and pastoral work hit a kind of "highway work zone." I needed to slow down, pay closer attention, and mind the new construction. The new construction, in my own thinking, was aided greatly by the work of psychologist Richard Schwartz, the founder of Internal Family Systems (IFS) therapy. I read everything about IFS that I could get my hands on. And soon enough, I found my way into the San Francisco clinical office of Jay Earley, a leading thinker and practitioner in IFS, and I did the therapeutic work myself.[6]

At this point I was already familiar with a variety of different styles of pastoral care, clinical counseling, and spiritual direction, but IFS proved to be an altogether different and more profitable experience. I'd had some therapists who focused on reframing my cognitive thoughts and others who focused on my early relationships with my parents. I'd yelled at my (imaginary!) mother in an empty chair and journaled through exercises using both my right and my left hand to access different parts of my psyche. But before IFS, I'd never experienced a process so clear, so accessible, and so immediately helpful.

IFS identifies four major components of our inner life: *Self, Protectors, Exiles, and Firefighters.* We're already familiar with the

True Self, which IFS simply identifies as Self.[7] The True Self is our core, our Inner Conductor, our guide. In IFS, True Self is characterized by care, compassion, curiosity, clarity, calmness, confidence, creativity, courage, and connectedness.[8] The other three components require a bit more elaboration. So let's look at these and see how they work within us, and explore how we might experience compassion from God ministering through our deepest Self.

PROTECTORS

According to IFS, parts of us evolved to compensate and course-correct for us.[9] Our remarkably complex brain is able to compartmentalize, so to speak. Certain parts of us become Protectors, playing a kind of managerial and self-protective role in our inner system.

Earlier I mentioned the Inner Critic. The Inner Critic is one type of Protector. Inner Critics may develop in order to remind us not to blow a big talk we need to give, or not to fail as a parent. Protectors can take on an almost infinite number of appearances, emotions, and forms. I've seen them emerge in some of the following guises:

The Fighter: A part that might appear with fists raised as if to say, "You'll need to fight me to get to her"

The Policeman: A part that reminds you of the rules you need to follow

The Helper: A part that might protect you by helping others

The Competent One: A part that works really hard to succeed so that you don't have to experience failure or shame

From a more pessimistic angle, these Protectors may be seen as defense mechanisms. And of course there are protective parts of us that blame-shift and avoid, push and react angrily. But we're invited, through IFS, to become curious about them.[10] I particularly like this aspect of IFS. You see, as a therapist I was trained in a whole host of ways to notice people's defenses and get around them. I also became adept at confronting them. But IFS is far more compassionate. IFS asks us to honor every part of ourselves, to become curious about every part's story, its origins, its fears and concerns.

> Notice a part of you that gets defensive or reactive. Instead of beating yourself up or shaming yourself about it, become curious. What role does this part of you play? Might it reveal anything to you about what it fears might happen if it didn't play this role?

As I've mentioned, I have a very obsessive part of me. It kicks in when I feel out of control, whether I'm behind on a deadline or late for a meeting or not as informed as I need to be. In these instances, I can become passive-aggressive or simply mean to those around me, including my family. And when I'm obsessive, I exhaust myself. I immerse myself in whatever I feel I need to do to get on top of things and maintain control. I can't rest. I can't relax my grip.

For years I beat myself up over this part of me. I tried to stop it. I used different things to relax — alcohol, exercise, getting away. But eventually I needed to greet this inner stranger. And so, in and through IFS, I began to pay attention to this obsessive part of me. I became curious. I wondered within about its story. I even got a sense of what it looked like, and I saw fear in its eyes.

"What are you scared of?" I asked it one day while I sat in a coffee shop, plagued by anxiety over what I'd failed to accomplish that morning. I could write another chapter on what I heard in response to my question. I heard shame. I heard fear. It turns out that this obsessive part of me keeps life ordered because I'm scared of failing, hate feeling ashamed, and fear rejection.

What I noticed, though, was that this obsessive, protective part of me became a bit less obsessive as I listened within to it. It became less powerful. It shrunk in stature. Strange as it seems, it's almost as if it felt understood. This happened as I let my deeper experience of God-within through my True Self express compassion and love toward it. I tangibly felt God peering at this part of me through my own deepest being, filled with tenderness and great interest.

> When you look inward, you may find several Protectors active at once. Each may need to spend a little time with you. As you acknowledge these Protectors, simply ask them if they'd be willing to allow YOU to lead. If you find yourself especially "stuck" in this process, find a therapist who can work with you.

And as the protective part of me relaxed, I relaxed, physically and emotionally. I became more present, and I was filled with sadness about how my obsessiveness hurts me and others I'm close to. I found myself quietly asking God to love it and forgive it for its twisted and compulsive ways. And as this part of me began to relax in grace, I expressed an even deeper curiosity within.

EXILES

Protectors play an important role in our inner world. They're like guards posted to protect vulnerable little children. And the vulnerable little children are Exiles.

Exiles are the most vulnerable parts of us. Sometimes we're triggered by a person or a situation which brings an Exile to the surface, eliciting pain or tears. But most of the time our Protectors make sure we can get along in life without being unduly impacted by our more painful exilic parts. Fortunately, dialogue with our Protectors can allow these parts to relax and let us, our True Selves, offer compassion, care, and healing through the Spirit to every broken part of us, including the Exiles.

I learned this through my IFS therapy. As the obsessive part of me relaxed, I recognized that it was actually protecting me from feeling shame. In fact, as I was internally attuned to this obsessive part, I could hear it whispering within, "You'll need to take care of that little boy." "That little boy" was me at four or five, hiding under the living-room side table. As I mentioned earlier, I could see him. As I continued this exercise, I could feel the pain of that little boy. It was tempting to become him, but I tried to stay in my True Self, allowing myself to feel the pain of the child but not to become the child. I could feel the grief in my body — my throat and my chest were tight, and I had tears in my eyes. Internally, I extended love and compassion to him, just as the father extended love and compassion to his prodigal son. I asked the little boy what he needed.

In these moments it's important to stay connected to your core, your True Self. Remember: the True Self, led by the Spirit, is the conductor of the orchestra. And the Protectors

> will relax only if they know you're leading. An Exile needs
> you to care for it, not to become it. Imagine loving it like a
> parent loves a hurting child. Ask it what it needs from you
> and from God.

Our Exiles need different things. Each carries a burden, and each feels pain in a different way. Each needs God in a different way (which makes me thankful that God reveals himself in so many different ways — as father, mother, refuge, rock, shepherd, rescuer, pursuer, desert guide). Over the years I've identified many protective and exilic parts of me, and each looks and feels different. It's important to avoid applying a universal Band-Aid in this situation; the goal is to exercise a new curiosity each time we go within to do this work.

A number of years ago I worked with a client who felt something profoundly traumatic well up within her on her wedding night. The intimate touch of her husband led to a surge of body memories — sensations of feeling dirty and ashamed. She recoiled from her husband and curled up in the fetal position on the bed, weeping. This painful experience made my client realize that she needed to do some significant work in therapy. Her body had clearly revealed something to her that her mind wasn't aware of. And although the prospect of doing the necessary work was scary and disturbing, she entered into it courageously and experienced great healing.

What we've learned from neurobiology is that our brains have a unique ability to compartmentalize pain. Sometimes we may not even have a clear mental recollection of a trauma, but our bodies will remember it.

When we address this trauma, it can sometimes feel like the inner work that's required is causing further fragmentation within us, especially when we feel overwhelmed. But for this client, for me, and for countless others, turning compassionately and lovingly toward every broken part of us actually brings about wholeness and connection. It may not feel that way all the time, but living from our core cultivates the freedom we long for.

FIREFIGHTERS

Let's assume for a moment that an exilic part of you has been triggered by a situation or someone's comment. Your body reflects the intense shame you feel. Your face flushes red and burns. Your heart begins to hammer mercilessly. Your palms sweat, and your mouth feels like the Sahara.

We've all had experiences like this, and when we do, we might feel like we're losing it. No amount of inner attentiveness seems to help; in fact, the process seems impossible precisely because we're triggered. This is the time when a Firefighter may appear to douse the blaze of shame.

Firefighters are still another part of us, a part that can enter our consciousness with a fury through behaviors like cutting or binging, (sometimes) purging or masturbating, or, at worst, suicide. Firefighters, like Protectors and Exiles, aren't bad — they're just misguided. Imagine that a tuba player in your inner orchestra decides that things simply aren't going well. So he stands up, gets the other players' attention, and shouts, "Follow my lead!" This disruption throws the entire orchestra into chaos.

In the same way, these parts of us feel like they're taking over. I once worked with a man who regularly cut himself. The behavior seemed absurd to his wife, who told him, "Just stop it. It's stupid." But something within him compelled him to hurt himself during those times when his inner pain and shame were triggered. His Firefighter was trying to help him.

But our Firefighters aren't simply those in-the-moment, reactive parts of us. Firefighters can also be keen and crafty, plotting ways of self-soothing. I worked with a pastor who was, at his core, a very good man. But he was plagued by intense shame. Most of the time his Protectors led the way, allowing him to preach and teach and counsel. But a Firefighter we ended up calling the Seducer would sometimes take over. When this happened, he'd find his way to a bar to seduce a woman, plotting his moves carefully and stealthily in order to protect his secret life.

Firefighters require both our curiosity and our compassion. Working with them often exposes the ashamed and traumatized Exiles within us. As Firefighters relinquish their need to control or numb our pain, they can become powerful champions of our health. They often have a fierce energy. One client of mine viewed a Firefighter he had as a disturbed metal-band drummer that, in health, became a powerful motivator whose energies turned toward caring for victims of molestation.

When his wife finally discovered his secret, the pastor couldn't believe what he'd done. I remember him saying to me, "It feels like my mind and my body were invaded by something else." We began working with his inner orchestra, and it became clear that he had been disconnected from his True Self for his entire life. He lived and moved through the world by putting on and taking off different masks. But the pain he was covering was most devastating. Through our work together he remembered that he had been sexually molested by an older female cousin when he was in early elementary school. And he discovered that the consequence was a distrust and hatred of women in general, and the fuel behind the Firefighter's fury.

What's fascinating is that this man was a typical exhausted pastor who complained often to his wife about people in the congregation, who resented the neediness of others, and who wavered in and out of depression.

What's true for so many of us is that we can function on a daily level while coping with some significant pain within, hardly aware of our inner war. And yet each of us has the opportunity to extend a gaze of grace within, inviting every broken part of us into wholeness in the Spirit.

Compassion for Every Part of Ourselves

The elusive wholeness we long for comes as we extend grace and love and compassion to every stranger within us. As every part of us relaxes, our entire being enters into its desired rest. We experience new energy, new resiliency, and a more lasting joy.

As I mentioned earlier, I found myself in a season of frequent travel while I was writing this book. My previous book's release made a number of groups eager to have me speak to them, and while I said no quite often, I did say yes to some exciting opportunities that came my way. In the course of two months, I traveled to eight different places. My suitcase stayed open in the bedroom at home, and my wife and I sometimes wondered whether I was coming or going.

I used the time as a kind of personal experiment. I asked myself, "Can I remain attentive to my inner orchestra even amid the hectic travel schedule, the anxiety of speaking, and the longing to be with my family?" I realized that we can dupe ourselves into believing that wholeness can be achieved only through some sort of monastic or ascetic existence, where we sit perpetually in the yoga position minding our being with utter attentiveness. But this isn't real life. It's true that our wholeness is cultivated in quiet and mindful times, but it's also cultivated in the frantic and frazzling moments — racing to pick up the kids from school on time, cleaning up the dog's mess, waiting out a flight delay. Wholeness is experienced as we attend to ourselves with care in every circumstance.

During my travels I noticed that I experienced times of almost zen-like attentiveness in my soul. I felt alive and free and present. I'd smile at angry flight attendants, engage my hosts in various places with great openness, and open my heart in prayer for those who would spontaneously come to mind. But then there were the out-of-balance times. There was the week where I had to speak and felt so out-of-body that I could hardly remember what I'd spoken about a few days later. There was the night I had too many martinis at the hotel bar and endured a morning-after headache. There was one speaking event that made me feel so panicky that I desperately tried to figure out how to get out of it. There was the flight where I felt merged with a very angry part of myself, and I gritted my teeth and heaped judgment on everyone sitting around me. But during these times, whether I was at 45,000 feet or in an uncomfortable retreat-center bed, I remembered my practice. I'd take a deep breath, descend back into my body, and feel at home.

I'll often imagine these various parts of me in a kind of inner living room of my soul. An exhausted part of me hogs the couch, scrambling for the remote. A busily obsessive part of me types away at the desk. A rebellious part of me concocts a scheme to disrupt someone. A frightened part of me hides under a side table. I'm sure that some of this sounds familiar to you — because you probably have some of the same kinds of inner experiences that I do. But in times of wholeness, we enter the inner living room in the Spirit with arms wide open, welcoming all of the parts of ourselves, asking for their attention, inviting them to relax.

In these moments of wholeness, we are fully present — present to what we're feeling, present to what we're saying, present to what we're seeing, present to who we're being. And people around us feel the difference. They feel the lightness of our being. They sense that we're connected — to ourselves, to the Spirit, to them, to all of creation. They see love, joy, peace, patience, kindness, goodness, faithfulness, gentleness, and self-control — the reality that our True Self is, quite literally, in control.

This is the elusive wholeness we long for.

Exercise 1: Getting to Know a Part of You

Perhaps while reading this book you've discovered a part of you that plays a fairly prominent role in your everyday life. Maybe it's the competent you that you put on at work, or the resourceful you that you bring to a committee meeting. Maybe it's the heroic you that squelches your needs so that you can take care of the kids, the spouse, the home, the bills. Whatever it is, take some time to get to know it. Maybe you see an image of it, and maybe you'd like to draw that image. Maybe there's a feeling associated with it — anxiety, sadness, angry determination. Maybe you feel it in your body — your neck hurts, your stomach is in knots, your head aches. Maybe it's sending you a clear message (Get your act together!).

Take a few moments to simply acknowledge its presence. Welcome it. Maybe you can say, "I'd like to get to know you a bit better." Be aware that you might not have totally positive feelings toward this part of you, so acknowledge those other feelings and allow yourself to grow in compassion and curiosity for this part. What does it want to communicate about how it feels, what it does, the role it plays, how it protects you, how it seeks to help you? Simply be present to it. You don't need to fix it, eliminate it, or control it. You just need to welcome the stranger and befriend it.

Exercise 2: God and a Part of You

Again, identify a part of you, perhaps even the one you worked with in the first exercise. How does this part of you experience God? Does it trust God? What might it need from God? Is it exhausted — and can God, perhaps, take over its exhausting role within you so that you don't have to be "on" all the time? Does it need God in a particular way (as father, mother, rock, friend, spouse, someone to hold you, someone to listen to you, etc.)? Try to determine this in order to give this part of you what it really needs.

embracing sweet communion

Tear off your masks. The church was not meant to be a masquerade.

CHARLES SPURGEON

Everyone who lives as a Christian in the Church, objectively and sacramentally, must also and of necessity hear the word: the Eucharist demands contemplation. The Christian's existence as a tabernacle demands that he exists as a hearer of the word. If he is to cherish the word within him, he must attend to the word which is above him.

HANS URS VON BALTHASAR

The more we get what we now call "ourselves" out of the way and let Him take us over, the more truly ourselves we become.

C. S. LEWIS

I AM A CHRISTIAN. This is how I've identified myself for as long as I can remember. For better or for worse, for richer or for poorer, this is my family — the family I was born into, the family

I was baptized into, the family I commune with, the family I'll be buried with.

Like any family, we have our dysfunctions and divisions. We can be mean and manipulative. We shame and blame in the name of Jesus. We talk about sin but remain alarmingly out of touch with our own darker sides, projecting our own unreconciled divisions outward.

In fact, we're masters of division. In and out. Believer and unbeliever. Right and wrong. Good and bad. Elect and reprobate. Clean and unclean. We've inherited categories, but we've created many more — to label, to include and to exclude. We've got lots of practice in the art of division, even though St. Paul came with a message of reconciliation of such polarization.

Given how much practice we've had, you'd think we'd agree on our own categories. Yet, when we "come together," we really don't. Sunday mornings remain the most racially, ethnically, and economically segregated time of the week. Divisive issues continue to create conflict. And as for the number of denominations and alliances — who can keep count anymore?

We are far from whole, both as individuals and as a body of believers. And our divisiveness is spiritually exhausting, sapping the Spirit-life and energy meant to enliven and enrich souls.

> How have you experienced division in the church? What particular divisions have affected you? What divisions have you perpetuated? If you haven't been part of a church, what is your perception of Christians? Do you think of them as divided? As divisive?

Sadly, some leave the church. The well-known novelist Anne Rice made headlines in 2010 when she left organized religion. I'm sure that many followed her lead. And I recall the times I've considered doing the same, times when exhaustion or embarrassment or resignation so permeated my spirit that leaving seemed to be a path to freedom.

But I didn't do it. And I can't do it. You see, splitting and dividing in whatever form never brings about wholeness, personally or corporately.[1] I've stayed, not only to be a pastor who leads others into wholeness, but in order to recognize my own inner dividedness — exposed through my own judgments, criticisms, and polarizations — and try to heal it. Community reveals our inner divisions in ways that solitary self-reflection cannot.

> Have you recognized your own dividedness in community? What aspects of yourself did you need to confront because of this? As a result, did you become more whole as an individual? As a believer?

In staying, I'm continuing to have to face myself.

In staying, I'm invited into new patterns that counter my exhausting ones.

In staying, I'm confronted with my own limitations, not least because I'm in a diverse community of people in whom I see my own best and worst.

In staying, I'm saying that I can't be made whole in isolation. I need you, and you need me.

In staying, I find my best chance of becoming whole and holy, of becoming wholehearted. And I believe we all do.

Disruptions in Union

When the disparate parts of my soul seem endlessly in conflict and my life's patterns become addictive and obsessive and self-consumed, I find my way back to church. When my own attempt to narrate happiness and wholeness for myself goes hopelessly off-course, I find my way back to church. When my own inner light seems dim and I can't find my way back to union, I find my way back to church.

When I was a child attending Peace Lutheran Church with my mom and dad, I'd sometimes stare at a reddish-hued candle near the center of the sanctuary. It was sometimes called the "Eternal Light," and I often stared at it for the entire hour. In the dim sanctuary amid the pastor's droning, that candle was a fixed point, a center. No doubt I'd doodle on a piece of scrap paper or hassle my sister, too. But I'd inevitably return to the light.

Our pastor — the pastor who baptized me and my sister and got my parents to come to church again — left this church. Even more radically, he left to become a rabbi. This was the first taste of division I can remember. And it hurt. In fact, this break in the very foundation of my childhood faith would reverberate for decades.

As all divisions do, this one led to long meetings and late-night conversations and fights over the vision of the church. Even though I was only in elementary school, I can remember my parents talking long and hard about this as I listened in, unsure how to process it all. Division damages the soul of the individual and the soul of a church, and it left scars on my little soul.

And other divisions and dysfunctions followed from this one. Subsequent pastors met with various levels of approval and disapproval from my parents, and they ended up taking our family to a smorgasbord of churches before I left for college. No doubt they'd been hurt by our pastor-turned-rabbi as well.

Still, our family stayed at Peace Lutheran Church for a while. And the candle remained lit.

Each Sunday we walked back in through the big double doors to its glow. Each Sunday this was the first thing I looked for. And I kept looking at it, captivated by its steadiness amid my own inner fears, by its consistency in the midst of my family's inconsistency.

It always seemed as if God was looking back at me.

(When I visited that church again a few decades later, the candle was the first thing I looked for. It wasn't there; it had been replaced by the technology of a modern worship band. But I didn't grieve. That candle had become a part of me. I had internalized it as a fixed point, an inner light, a calm and steady center that in time would become my own amid confusion, exhaustion, and division.)

When I was in the fifth grade, my parents chose a new church for our family: Trinity Lutheran. At that point the Lutherans decided I was old enough to take a communicants class. I remember the class being held in the choir loft, a balcony with an enormous pipe organ at the back of the church — the church without an eternal light. During each class, I'd stare down at the altar, wondering why on earth a church wouldn't have an eternal light. My eyes would dart back and forth, looking for something to center myself.

It was in fifth grade that I began to find this new center: the Eucharist — the very thing that my communicants class was preparing me for. The pastor's teaching hadn't impacted me much, but Communion did.

Back then, my dad might complain about the pastor's preaching, my mom might complain about my dad's complaining, and my sister and I might complain about the length of the service, but as I recall no one ever complained about Communion. Bread and wine. Body and blood. Christ dying, Christ rising, Christ coming again. We all knew enough to recognize the sacred when we saw it.

At my first Communion, I took a large gulp of port wine from the chalice, a sensation I'll always remember — my throat burned as my face flushed. That first rush of heat to my cheeks seemed to wake something up inside of me. Even now, my recollection isn't visual or auditory — it's physical. *My body felt it.* It may have been my first realization that God wanted me not just to know him but to feel him. It felt like that wine permeated every part of me before the warmth finally subsided. Maybe God was permeating every atom of my being?

And what's more, something in this sacred act *felt rebellious* — the church let me do something that the state said I couldn't do until I was twenty-one. Drinking from that cup seemed like a revolutionary act, something I'd later learn it is in a deeper way. But the lesson I learned was enough for a fifth-grader. God, it seemed, wasn't as "uptight" as I'd thought. Maybe God was bigger and better than I had imagined?

Eventually I would know my new center — but not quite yet. I realized that even as people gathered to kneel around the rails of Trinity Lutheran's altar, they weren't magically changed. People are people. My tradition calls us *simul iustus et peccator* — simultaneously just and sinful. And we'd prove our sinfulness time and time again. As a sensitive kid, I'd feel the weight of other people's issues acutely, which would often push me off-center.

> What are your stories of disappointment and division? How do you think they've affected your spiritual life? Your life with the church?

And there were fights — always fights. I remember my dad arguing with other church leaders over how they interpreted the

Bible or diagnosed the problems of the church or understood the shifting tides of 1970s and 1980s church culture, with its new and mysterious charisms. I'll always remember the old Dutch elder who, as we were leaving his church, proclaimed with great conviction in a thick Dutch brogue, "This is the *true* church."

And there were scandalous things, too. It seemed the church wasn't immune to the things it protested against. My first exposure to pornography was at the home of a church leader who kept his "dirty" magazines in, of all places, the bottom of a laundry basket in the main bathroom. An elder in one of my churches had an affair with the organist and murdered his wife, a scandal that would find its way to Court TV in its first days.

And there was pain. Youth group wasn't always the safe-for-your-kids place it was advertised to be. The kids in church could be just as cruel as the kids at my public school.

Through it all, I kept on going to church. And while my parents flipped through the ecclesial remote control looking for just the right church, I kept looking for the light, for the bread, for the wine, and for that full-bodied union I longed for. Amid the dysfunction and division, there was always union.

Liturgical Therapy

Among the different hats that I wear, "therapist" might just be my favorite. I love teaching and writing, but something extraordinary happens behind the closed doors of the therapist's inner sanctum. What I've witnessed as real transformation in people's souls has, quite often, happened in the uniquely vulnerable and sacred space of the therapeutic relationship.

People who have experienced this intimacy will often ask me why church can't be more like therapy. I've had addicts say that their weekly meetings are far more intimate and life-giving and real than church. I've heard clients say that they've never felt safe in church because pastors seem to want to add burdens that only exhaust them. Many lament that they don't see the Jesus who says, "Come to me, all you that are weary and are carrying heavy burdens, and I will give you rest" (Matt. 11:28). In fact, the Jesus they encounter seems a little ticked off that they're not doing more for him.

I can't fix this, but I'd like to offer my own pathway to wholeness and wholeheartedness that doesn't circumvent the church. Indeed, I've seen something far more transformational occur in those who've discovered their own stories caught up in the larger Story of God, among those who've seen the liturgical expressions of worship open them to participating in a life larger than their own. In using the word "liturgy," I'm not talking about something dark, ritualistic, or stoic. No, I'm imagining the classic and ancient life-giving liturgical patterns entered into daily and weekly, and also those patterns that mark time, patterns that invite us back to our center in God.

At this point you might be thinking, *Oh, here it comes — he's going to end the book by saying that the answer to my exhaustion and busyness is going to church.* Let me answer this first with a definitive "No." I've watched many people go to church week after week and experience no transformation, no wholeness, and even more division. I've served Communion to people who've walked back to their seats and gone back to their same old patterns. And when I'm not living whole and holy, I'm one of these people. Just "going to church" isn't the answer. What we're after is *union and communion — truly "being the church" together.* And our own Inner Light brightens in the company of other lights, in a community of women and men who participate in the Great Story together.

Here's a metaphor that helps me. When I was first learning

to play an instrument, my dad gave me a metronome, a wooden, pyramid-shaped device. We could wind it up to a particular speed, and its ticking sound would keep me in rhythm, setting a beat I could play to. Of course, in my early days of playing, I'd be all over the place, unable to keep that beat, unable to find the rhythm. But eventually I'd find myself playing trombone in a big band where it was sometimes my job to set the beat in songs that demanded the loud, booming quarter notes of a bass instrument. I could do it because I had learned what the metronome was designed to teach me: I could feel the beat, like the ticking of an internal clock.

The liturgy offers us the beat, gets us back in tune with the cosmic harmony, takes us out of our old, life-leeching patterns just long enough to allow us to hear the whisper of God saying, "Where are you? Come home to me."

You know what I'm talking about. Often we're trying to become whole apart from God. We look to a thousand other things or people offering personal fulfillment or self-esteem. But C. S. Lewis points out that God is the one who makes us truly whole:

> The more we get what we now call "ourselves" out of the way and let Him take us over, the more truly ourselves we become. There is so much of Him that millions and millions of "little Christs," all different, will still be too few to express Him fully. He made them all. He invented — as an author invents characters in a novel — all the different [people] that you and I were intended to be. In that sense our real selves are all waiting for us in Him. It is no good trying to "be myself" without Him. The more I resist Him and try to live on my own, the more I become dominated by my own heredity and upbringing and surroundings and natural desires. In fact what I so proudly call "Myself" becomes merely the meeting place for trains of events which I never started and which I cannot stop. I am not, in my natural state, nearly so much of a person as I like to believe: most of what I call "me" can be very easily explained. It is when I turn

to Christ, when I give myself up to His Personality, that I first begin to have a real personality of my own.[2]

Lewis's point is clear: I can't find "me" in isolation, as convenient as that might be. I can't find "me" in a new app, as handy as that would be. No, my deepest me is buried with Christ in God and is waiting for me at my center, where the Inner Light shines brightly.

The great tradition of the church, although it's marred by the twisted egos and strategies of God's people, offers three pathways to union. Note that these are just pathways, not the end goal. They are where we find hints of God, where we taste graces from God.

PATHWAY ONE: DAILY PRESENCE IN PRAYER

Daily presence in prayer means attending, every day and throughout the day, to God. This may seem like a hopeless pipe dream. Given our scattered and fragmented lives, who has time to practice the presence of God throughout the day, even in ordinary ways? We can barely squeeze in a morning devotion!

There are, in fact, many pathways to daily prayer.[3] It's best if we don't get caught up in ranking these different pathways as "better" or "worse." We need to recognize that our personalities and needs are different, and that our racial, ethnic, and cultural identities intersect deeply with these very personal practices. These critical factors make it unwise to promote "a" practice as if it's "the" practice.

Still, given the direction of this book and my conviction that our fragmentation keeps us at a distance from God and ourselves, I want to share a particular pathway that has become important for me. Some call it contemplative prayer. As such, it's distinguished from more active prayer practices that employ various techniques, words, and images. Contemplative prayer invites us into silence — uncomfortable silence. It invites us to attend to the disparate parts of ourselves and surrender each to God's loving embrace, which frees us to enjoy sweet communion with God. It invites us to relinquish words and images for simple and free presence to God.

My favorite sixteenth-century Reformer is actually a Spanish mystic, St. Teresa of Ávila, a brilliant writer, spiritual director, Reformer, monastery planter, and strategist. Her greatest work, *The Interior Castle,* details a journey from fragmentation to wholeness in a process she calls *recollection.*[4] Drawing from the writings of another Spanish mystic, Francisco de Osuna, she employs an idea that has extraordinary psychological relevance today: the idea that we, quite literally, need to be re-collected.

To simplify, this way of prayer invites us to be ever mindful of who we are and where we are in the present moment, a hard proposition when we're mired in a past regret or lost in future-tripping. But this practice has the power to re-center us, to re-collect us. One version of it encourages us to use a key prayer word like "Love" or "Jesus" or "Come" to invite the Spirit back into our immediate, lived experience until we no longer need the word.[5] Others simply ask us to become deeply acquainted with silence, entering into solitude (with all its noise!) in order to quiet our anxieties, surrender our immediate concerns, and relax into sweet communion with God.[6]

As a leader of silent retreats, I often find that this practice is hard — hard for me, hard for the participants, and even harder for introverts than extroverts. Asking an extrovert to be silent for 24 to 48 hours is like asking a bird not to fly! But the introvert often faces a greater challenge: listening to inner noise that is fierce and relentless. Recently an extrovert told me, "The first hour was tough, but then it became a gift." An introvert said, "The first hour was beautiful, but then it became a battle." Either way, in a culture of noise we are usually profoundly uncomfortable with silence.

And so our first challenge is to begin the practice, as difficult as that might be. We don't need to do it perfectly. Recollection or contemplation begins, quite simply, with intention. It begins with a mindful awareness of what is stirring within at this very moment. What we discover is that there are many obstacles to union — gripping thoughts that capture our attention, anxieties that nag at us, addictive behaviors that distract us. Contemplative prayer invites us both to notice these things and then to allow them to move along. So, clearly, our second challenge is to remain faithful in our practice. When we do, it becomes easier — and fulfilling at a very deep spiritual level.

The practice of quieting our being in contemplative prayer has evolved over time, but it's commended to us by none other than St. Augustine in a sermon on the Third Commandment. St. Augustine was aware of the peril of busyness, particularly mental busyness, manifesting itself in personal restlessness and relational discord:

> The third commandment enjoins quietness of heart, tranquility of mind. This is holiness. Because here is the Spirit of God. This is what a true holiday means, quietness and rest. Unquiet people recoil from the Holy Spirit. They love quarreling. They love argument. In their restlessness they do not allow the silence of the Lord's Sabbath to enter their lives. Against such restlessness we are offered a kind of Sabbath in the heart. As if God were saying "Stop being so restless, quieten the uproar in your minds. Let go of the idle fantasies that fly around in your head." God is saying, "Be still and see that I am God" (Ps. 46).[7]

With St. Augustine's blessing, we can enter into a regular practice ourselves.

My practice has evolved over time. Usually I pray for ten to twenty minutes twice a day. I sit upright in a chair and use deep breathing to center myself. Sometimes I'll begin with the Jesus Prayer:

Lord Jesus Christ [breathing in . . .],
Son of God [breathing out . . .],
have mercy on me [breathing in . . .],
a sinner [breathing out . . .].

Sometimes, echoing Augustine, I'll begin with Psalm 46:10: "Be still, and know that I am God." I begin with the entire verse, but slowly, while breathing deeply in and out, I remove a word or two until I end with "Be":

Be still, and know that I am God.
    Be still, and know that I am.
        Be still, and know.
            Be still.
                Be.

As I enter into the silence, I imagine myself descending down into my body. Too often I live disconnected from my body, lost in the cocktail party of my mind with its endless chatter. Descending into my body by using my breathing and my imagination allows me to find my center. Words fall away. The chatter fades away. And I can enjoy the sweetness of intimacy with a God who simply loves — yes, loves — being with me. And being with you.

St. Teresa of Ávila believed that our journey involved moving from the circumference of our lives to the center, where God eternally dwells. She imagined a journey through seven dwellings, each presenting us with unique obstacles to union, each with an invitation to greater depth. It's helpful for me to remember that at the very center of my being, God dwells. St. Augustine writes, "God is more intimate to me than I am to myself."[8] What he means is that God is already at our center, drawing us in. We need only listen. We need only trust our deepest longing. Teresa and Augustine, among others, believed that God's grace draws us into union.

Throughout the day, and particularly when I'm awakened to my distracted state, I take a deep breath. I've come to realize that I don't often breathe fully and deeply unless I'm winded after a good exercise session. Now, I recognize the distracted moment for what it is. Maybe I'm stewing about something my older daughter did that ticked me off. Maybe I'm obsessing about what will happen on my Netflix show. Maybe I'm anxiously preparing for a lecture. In these moments, I stop. I breathe deeply. I whisper to the fragmented parts of myself, "It's going to be OK. Relax." And I feel myself come back together. I awaken again to the reality that God is at the center. I find myself in God. Awake and alert, I continue on.

> Does your daily practice of prayer move you beyond words into a lived presence with God? If not, what might you be able to change about your praying to make it more meaningful?

Be still, and know that I am God.

Practicing the presence of God is, indeed, a practice, but it is a graced practice. If you long for it, your intentions will meet the astounding grace of a God who is presently drawing you into communion. You will notice your obstacles. But you'll also notice hints of the transcendent. Many of these hints are wonderfully gratifying in themselves, echoes of a union we all long for. We sense these echoes in the glance of a friend, a good glass of wine, a sunset over the lake, a late-night conversation with a kindred spirit, the large oak tree that raises its arms in praise. We're drawn into the infinite love of a God who is infinitely wooing us into union, even through these small things. They are moving us toward our ultimate goal.

And so I encourage you to use the resources cited in this chapter. Exercise your curiosity. Trust your deep longing for wholeness, and recognize that fragmentation is not the final word. Right now, take a moment to breathe deeply and be grateful for how God relentlessly pursues, inviting you to more and more love, more and more sweet communion. The peace you long for amid the busyness is possible. Your heart will guide you there, but it is where the Guide resides.

PATHWAY TWO: WEEKLY PARTICIPATION IN THE STORY

Since the very beginning of the faith, Christians have worshiped on the first day of the week as a way of participating in the Story of God. I'm using the word "participating" deliberately, because many today might view worship as an "experience" or a time to "know" God. It's certainly true that knowing and experiencing God are part and parcel of Christian worship. But worship is active — it involves us just as much as it involves God. That's why Christians use the liturgy, a word that means "the work of the people."[9]

This work isn't exhausting. In fact, it's supposed to be a bit like waking out of our slumber and discovering a Great Feast that's ours to enjoy. Worship is where we find life in and among others whose Inner Lights, like ours, have been dimmed by life's stresses. It's the place where we're welcomed back to our center, our story, our very selves.

A classic liturgy might begin with the call to worship, which often includes a responsive reading through which we acknowledge our desire to meet God. This call is much like God hosting us and welcoming us back into our deeper story, our greater life. It's not a perfunctory "welcome to church" but a rich, often participatory call-and-response:

Leader: The Lord be with you.
People: And also with you.

Think about that. The first words of the week, spoken to our dimmed Inner Lights and weary spirits, are these: "The Lord be with you." They remind us of union, of our fundamental wholeness found in a life flowing within.

Christian worship also includes confession, which might seem strange and antiquated. Many churches today completely eliminate this part of the liturgy, largely because any mention of sin can be off-putting to worshipers. I understand that completely. The way that sin is talked about is often harsh and shaming. In fact, I've heard pastors talk about sin as if it's our most fundamental reality, and about God as profoundly disappointed in us, as waiting for us to get our acts together before singing songs to him. If this is confession, count me out. But I see it differently. And thankfully, I think that, for the most part, Jesus and the church throughout history see it differently too. Confession is our opportunity to identify obstacles to union. In solidarity with others, we are able to name our false selves individually or together, and reconnect to our *big-D* Desire for God. Confession paves the way to wholeness, to wholeheartedness.

And this is why absolution — the assurance of pardon — follows. It names God's commitment to us, extending grace even amid our self-sabotage. Grace is God's response. God moves toward us, not away from us. God offers compassion, not judgment. At the center of Christian worship are the reality of the cross and the resurrection of Jesus, which ended any false notion of an angry or violent God. In a vivid display of self-giving, God showed us just how committed he is to our wholeness.

The homily or sermon often follows. This isn't meant to be a forty-five-minute diatribe about who's in and who's out, but a verbal testimony to the Story's central character, Jesus, and his work of reconciling all things within and without. Today the homily has become a self-help chat in certain contexts and a doctrinal diatribe in others. But, as someone who preached weekly for a few years and many times after that, I see the homily as the opportunity to tell the biblical stories of other men and women who wrestled with life in God. And most of all, this is where pastors offer verbal testimony to the One who bridged the gap — Jesus — whose very being as fully God and fully human provides the ultimate picture of a divided cosmos made whole. Jesus is central because Jesus is Wholeness among us, the incarnate God embodying, abiding, suffering, dying, and re-merging from death's door of division to make all things new.

> What is it like for you to understand weekly worship in this way? How might it kindle — or rekindle — deeper participation on your part?

Weekly Christian worship, as it has been practiced for centuries, often includes a celebration of the Eucharist or Communion, the center of the participatory experience and the very apex of contemplative union and communion with God in communal worship. Again, the liturgy begins with these words:

Leader: The Lord be with you.
People: And also with you.

It's as if we can't hear it and say it enough. And while Communion might seem to some like an empty or antiquated ritual, it has been a way for Christians throughout the centuries to feast on their deepest life in God, to experience "God with us." The earthy elements of bread and wine reconnect us to our bodies, to our humanity, to this world. We're reminded that we, like the bread, are taken by God, blessed by God, broken, and given to the world for its flourishing. We eat and drink grace, wholeness, and life to be conduits of this life to others.

In worship, Christians also pray the Lord's Prayer and/or recite an ancient creed to testify to the faith. Again, these are expressions of the faith that have been commended by others and used throughout the centuries; they are signs of unity and participation in the church throughout the ages. They become living testimonies of a faith centered in and on the reconciling and whole-making work of Jesus for the sake of all. And for St. Paul, it seems that "all" means "all":

> For in him all the fullness of God was pleased to dwell, and through him God was pleased to reconcile to himself all things, whether on earth or in heaven, by making peace through the blood of his cross. (Col. 1:19-20)

Jesus seems to be in the business of reconciling all divisions, even cosmic divisions.

An offering is also taken, partly so that the church can pay its bills (which is critical to its ongoing work), and partly to support the ongoing mission of reconciling all people and all things. Once again, this ritual invites our participation. In giving, we experience the freedom and wholeness God longs for us to enjoy. Giving actually helps us to detach ourselves from those things we've been clinging to, to hold our possessions more loosely, and to trust a bit more. And our resources go to the work of reconciling all things, beginning locally, beginning in our very own neighborhoods, where racism and social status and polarizing political opinions tear at the fabric of wholeness.

Christian worship ends with a benediction, a good word, a blessing, an invitation to go out into the world as ambassadors of God's reconciling work. We all long for a blessing. Who of us didn't long for Mom or Dad to say, "I'm proud of you"? God's blessing is also a promise to go with us, to dwell with us, to be a conduit of his life through us to the world.

Can you see it? In this "work," we're invited back to ourselves in Christ. In this worship, we're able to sing songs and pray prayers that extol God — not because God is some Holy Narcissist who needs it but because we're reconnected to the original *shalom* flourishing we were made in and for. We're recognizing God for who God really is — not the Transcendent Bully, but the One who puts an end to that in Jesus, who ends our violence and our pain, and who welcomes us into a new reality of faith, hope, and love. Worship helps make us whole and holy.

Pathway Three: A Yearly Story-Cycle

Christians also find themselves immersed in a yearly Story, which begins a new cycle every fall. The Christian new year isn't January 1; it begins with Advent. During this time, we long for God's life to come to earth as it is in heaven, looking ahead to Christmas as that great hope. Following Christmas, Christians celebrate Epiphany in early January, remembering the appearance of the wise men to Jesus, the climax of the twelve days of Christmas that culminates in the celebration of Jesus as King. Again, the rhythm is clear: God wants us to long for and celebrate his being-with-us, his nearness, his reconciling work of making us whole and holy.

Several weeks later, Ash Wednesday marks the beginning of the season of Lent. Though it's not observed in some contexts, Ash Wednesday is one of my favorite days of the year. I've had the privilege of putting ashes on the foreheads of men, women, and children and saying, "You are dust, and to dust you shall return." While this may sound morbid, it's actually deeply humanizing. It's about embracing our humanness, something we run from in our shame. It's about naming our limitations, something we resist in our perfectionism.

The season of Lent is a forty-day period (excluding Sundays) that invites us into an intentional time of self-reflection. Classically, it has been a time of instruction for those exploring Christian faith and preparing for Christian baptism. Baptism, the central initiatory rite of Christian life together, marks our union in a unique way, with its vivid picture of being plunged into and brought out of the deep waters, cleansed and washed in God. During Lent, Christians consider this baptismal identity, and they often give up something that's difficult for them to go without — whether it's social media or chocolate or coffee — in order to prompt a daily recollection of their deep dependence on God. The point is not, of course, to pick a behavior to embrace in order to please God. The point is to identify what keeps us from union, from connection, and from wholeness, and to commit during this forty-day period to removing obstacles to union.

How might the frantic and fragmented rhythms of your life change if you oriented your living around this story cycle? Think about how you might be able to make this cycle an integral part of your life.

In the week that ends Lent and leads up to Easter, we're reminded of the cost of reconciliation in Christ's sufferings. We're taken through the Triduum, three consecutive days of participating together in the central events around Christ's last days and death. We see what wholeness takes and what reconciliation costs. We see Jesus betrayed by a friend. We see the horrors of Roman imperialism and pharisaical exclusivism joined to do away with the life of the fully human God, the very beacon of wholeness and reconciliation, which is an offense to some. But in the first hours of Easter, Christians celebrate with a vigil, a baptismal service in which new life bursts forth out of the dark void. And with a new morning, we come together for the most significant holy day on the calendar, Easter, on which we discover that God's purposes of reconciliation cannot be thwarted. For the next fifty days, Christians celebrate the life of the resurrected Jesus and the new mission, one that will bring God closer to us than ever.

Pentecost celebrates this, recalling the first Pentecost, when God's Spirit was poured out on all, breaking the barriers of race and ethnicity, of gender and social status. Grace became universally available. And God sent — and sends — men and women to become ambassadors of this grace, proclaiming the reality that God is reconciling all things and all people in Jesus.

Until Advent, when the cycle begins again, Christians will live into the ordinary but extraordinary reality that they are dwelling places of God's Spirit, conduits of God's love, ambassadors of the reconciling work of a God who wants to bring heaven to earth.

These are the three pathways that Christians walk, not to fulfill mere duty or to perpetuate some outdated ritualism, but to embrace their life-giving possibilities for us and for all. Together, Christians are called to this reconciling life, reminded daily, weekly, and yearly of the Story in which it all coheres and the person around whom it's centered. These are pathways to wholeness and holiness, and although we Christians have done our very best to sabotage their life-giving purposes, we can listen to and participate in their rhythms again, with new hope and imagination.

Ambassadors of Shalom

At this point it's important to circle back to where we began — in the exhausting busyness of our daily lives that pull us to and fro in a thousand different directions. Surrounded by our electronic devices, hemmed in by schedules, spending precious hours in cars and on planes, we might feel like any chance at real, lasting wholeness must be reserved for monks and mystics. We might even dream of finding a monastery in a distant place, far away from inconsistent pastors and moody parishioners, far away from the ding of a new e-mail or the incessant ring of the cell phone.

I've had the same dream, and I suspect I always will. But the great masters of solitude, those monks and mystics who left cities to find wholeness in deserts and who left family to find union alone, are quite rare, and they wouldn't advocate that we follow the same path. Surprisingly, most took to the desert precisely because they were readying themselves to return to the wearying world they were called to serve. In solitude, they prepared themselves not to escape but to re-enter whole.

Few of us have this luxury. Even those of us who've studied at seminaries know that they're a far cry from the old monastic training centers, where prayer and solitude and deep inner work were required. It's tough to get away long enough to be at home in your True Self again. Most of our getaways, as I've said previously, just exhaust us more.

So the challenge today is to find wholeness right where we are — in the world, amid broken and divided souls like us, and in imperfect churches with imperfect pastors and imperfect singing and imperfect community. The challenge is to move into the dark places, both in our own hearts and in our own communities, and bring them light. And while we may separate from others for a time, we must recognize that wholeness never comes in isolation.

The first community envisioned in the Bible was God-community: Father and Son and Spirit, existing forever and ever in eternal, flourishing wholeness. As my Christian Story goes, God made this world to invite us into that wholeness, that oneness, experienced even amid different personalities. God, Three-in-One, knew this was possible. But we became adept at sabotaging it.

God offered the perfect Communion, experienced within Father and Son and Spirit, to human beings — indeed, to all of creation — which was made to live in harmony and wholeness, in *shalom,* according to the Hebrew Scriptures. *Shalom* was God's dream for the world, and it continues to be so. As the Story goes, God went to great lengths to restore *shalom,* to reconcile the polar opposites — Creator and creature, male and female, Jew and Gentile, master and slave.

Today's God-inspired reconciliation plays itself out as people commit to becoming whole and to becoming ambassadors of this wholeness, wherever they go, in the name of the reconciling God. As God sent the Son and as God and the Son sent the Spirit, so the Trinity sends us to invite others into wholeness, into *shalom.*

This is the Story that is proclaimed and enacted each Sunday. This is the Story, unchanging even though divided and unreconciled people like you and me twist it and misrepresent it.

God isn't at war. God is at peace. This was the reconciling, redeeming reality of the cross. The cross ended violence, making wholeness possible, sending reverberations of *shalom* through a groaning creation. In Jesus, God makes people hungry and thirsty again — hungry and thirsty for justice, particularly for those outside of the dividing walls. In Jesus, God makes us compassionate, and we take up the cause of the bruised and battered and cast aside. In Jesus, God reconciles every disparate part of our being in order to set our hearts single-mindedly on the cause of universal reconciliation.

And we become whole and holy precisely in the context where

God has us — in the factory or the software design company, at the grocery store or on a park bench, in our brilliance and in our absence of any cognitive capacity. God does this work in us and through us when we're on the subway and in our cars, when we're having dinner and when we're sleeping. We need not become monks. We need only find our Center, our Inner Light, and remain connected to it and to others connected to it, whether we're gathered around the Communion table, or at work or at play.

Being connected to others who long to live from their own Inner Light fosters wholeness and creates communities of people who seek to invite others into this life-giving wholeness.

It is astounding to hear stories of early Christian communities that practiced this life of wholeness. These stories give us hope that living as a whole and holy people might be possible. In an early second-century letter to Diognetus, one early witness says this about Christians:

> They dwell in their own countries, but simply as sojourners. As citizens, they share in all things with others, and yet endure all things as if foreigners. They marry, as do all [others]; they beget children; but they do not destroy their offspring. They have a common table, but not a common bed. They are in the flesh, but they do not live after the flesh. They pass their days on earth, but they are citizens of heaven. They obey the prescribed laws, and at the same time surpass the laws by their lives. They love all men, and are persecuted by all. They are unknown and condemned; they are put to death, and restored to life. They are poor, yet make many rich; they are in lack of all things, and yet abound in all; they are dishonored, and yet in their very dishonor are glorified.[10]

Even more astounding are the testimonies of those who hated Christians but were persuaded by their extraordinary lifestyles. An early second-century skeptic called Lucian writes,

For these poor wretches persuade themselves that they shall be immortal, and live for everlasting; so that they despise death, and some of them offer themselves to it voluntarily. Again, their first lawgiver taught them that they were all brothers, when once they had committed themselves so far as to renounce the gods of the Greeks, and worship that crucified sophist, and live according to his laws. So they hold all things alike in contempt, and consider all property common, trusting each other in such matters without any valid security.[11]

Another second-century skeptic who practiced law in ancient Rome offers a similar observation:

They had been accustomed to assemble on a fixed day before daylight and sing by turns a hymn to Christ as a god; and . . . they bound themselves with an oath, not for any crime, but to commit neither theft, nor robbery, nor adultery, not to break their word and not to deny a deposit when demanded.[12]

Of course, it would be a mistake to idealize any particular people or period of time. But it's amazing to see the impact of those who stand together, connected to the Inner Light, illumined for purposes beyond their own. They give us a taste of the life of wholeness and holiness that is possible, even for the church.

Time to Wake Up

The Christian Story, as I see it, is a story of union and communion, of wholeness and holiness. It tells us who we are. It gives us practices so that we can remain connected to it. It gives us a mission to connect others to it. As I see it, this is my task and yours until God makes all things new in the end.

Our exhaustion tells a different story. I began this book by acknowledging a quiet inner voice that accompanies us wherever we go, the voice of shame. That voice can be triggered at any moment, and shame's power can send us into a fury of activity, all in response to that dreaded question: "Am I enough?" We'll wear ourselves out trying to answer it. We'll look for something or someone to ground us, to anchor us, to make us feel important or happy or secure or successful or beautiful. We'll pursue perfecting ourselves at the cost of our health and our wholeness. This counter-story has become the dominant cultural story for the Western world, much to our detriment.

Our weariness tells of a fundamental disconnect. The life-light has become obscured. We've become disconnected from our deepest selves, alienated from the eternity of the present moment. In the oldest part of the Christian Story, the voice of shame is the voice of the Serpent, begging us to doubt our soul's Inner Light, its immeasurable dignity — begging us to doubt that we are enough.

In these moments, our divided souls can feel adrift at sea or, worse, pummeled by a storm. This is when our anxiety takes over, pushing us to charge harder. And our regrets overwhelm us, driving us to overcompensate to the point of exhaustion. Unsteadied, we try everything our culture insists can help. But nothing that we do works, because everything that we try takes us away from our center rather than to it, away from God rather than to God. We become legion — many — split and shattered to our core.

And so, in this desperate place, we listen for that still deeper voice within that whispers, "Where are you?" It's another question, and far closer to God's heart.

As we listen to this voice, this question, we become aware of a deep ache in our soul for reunion. We feel the brutal, terrifying effects of division deep down in our spirit, and we hunger and thirst for wholeness. We sense the discord among those we love, and we crave communion. We see the Father with arms open wide, saying, "Come home." We feel the rush of waters from the Inner Fountain, the wellspring of life, saying, "Drink deeply."

> Since rich store of every kind of good abounds in Christ, let us drink our fill from this fountain, and from no other.
>
> John Calvin

Thomas Merton puts it this way:

Christ [is] calling us to awake from sleep, to return from exile, and find our true selves within ourselves, in that inner sanctuary which is His temple and His heaven, and (at the end of the prodigal's homecoming journey) the "Father's House."[13]

We're called to wake up — to wake up to our true selves; to wake up to the kinds of patterns and practices that only breed disconnection in our souls; to wake up to the silly divisions we breed within and without; to wake up to the soul-numbing strategies for keeping our lives together that only pull us further apart. We're called to wake up to the ways in which we hide and avoid, just like Adam and Eve. We're called to wake up to God's *shalom* life in our souls and in our world, and to extend that wake-up call to all.

But we need to remember that God's invitation isn't an angry or coercive one. It's the same free invitation that Jesus extended to prostitutes and tax collectors, to know-it-alls and have-nots:

Come to me, all you that are weary and are carrying heavy burdens, and I will give you rest. (Matt. 11:28)

To come to Jesus is to come to wholeness, to the very center of ourselves, where Life and Light reside.

We also need to remember that the antidote to exhaustion isn't rest. It's wholeheartedness. A life of unity and union. A life undivided. Much has happened in your life and mine to cause dividedness. There is much in our churches and workplaces, in our politics and our family lives, which causes division. Sometimes it seems that division and fragmentation may have the last word.

But wherever you find yourself right now, the call is to wake up. To wake up to your deepest life. To wake up to what is most real in you and about you. To wake up from the slumber of resignation. To wake up to your fundamental unity and wholeness. To wake up to God's deepest Spirit-life within you, waiting to burst forth and to become your steady, strong, and stable center.

Yes, you and I feel pulled in a thousand different directions. But your answer isn't a better calendar program on your iPhone or another resolution in the new year. The answer is closer to you than you are. Your deepest life is already dwelling within. Your deepest life is there for you to feast upon. Fountains of living water are there to drink from.

And so, as you close this book, take a very deep breath. Find your center. Greet yourself. Greet God in you. Remember that you are not alone. Breathe again, taking in the Spirit-life that expands your whole being, equipping you for this moment, enabling you to live in the present, to be connected, clear, compassionate, and courageous. Filled to the brim, you will become one whose wholeness and holiness are contagious. You will discover a new capacity to be gracious, to yourself and to others. You will work hard, and be present in everything you do. And then you will rest, really rest, because you are whole and wholehearted.

Animated by this freedom, you'll be able to cry out with Gerard Manley Hopkins, "What I do is me: for that I came" — and mean it. It won't sound selfish. It will sound like you've recovered your heart, like you've come home to yourself. In fact, as we end this book together, it might be appropriate to let Hopkins offer you and me the last word, a last invitation to a flourishing life of wholeness and holiness. May it be a vision, a prayer, a place you return to in your ongoing journey back into your own life, the life that becomes Christ's life to a world desperate for wholeness.

Each mortal thing does one thing and the same:
Deals out that being indoors each one dwells;
Selves — goes itself; *myself* it speaks and spells,
Crying *What I do is me: for that I came.*

I say more: the just man justices;
Keeps grace: that keeps all his goings graces;
Acts in God's eye what in God's eye he is —
Christ — for Christ plays in ten thousand places,
Lovely in limbs, and lovely in eyes not his
To the Father through the features of men's faces.[14]

Notes

Notes to the Introduction

1. Dr. Seuss, quoted in David Kundtz, *Awakened Mind* (San Francisco: Conari Press, 2009), p. 208.

2. David Bohm, *Wholeness and the Implicate Order* (London: Routledge, 2005), pp. 236-38.

3. Brené Brown, *Men, Women, and Worthiness,* at http://www.soundstrue.com/store/men-women-and-worthiness-2911.html.

4. The audio CD is available at www.davidwhyte.com through Many Rivers Press, Langley, Washington.

5. David Whyte shares this story in written form in *Crossing the Unknown Sea*: find it at http://www.gratefulness.org/readings/whyte_dsr.htm.

6. I'm part of a group of men and women who form the Society for Christian Psychology. We have very lively conversations, in the context of the Christian tradition, about who we are and how we're made.

Notes to Chapter 1

1. David Letterman, *Parade* magazine, 26 May 1996, p. 6.

2. Brené Brown, *The Gifts of Imperfection* (Center City, Minn.: Hazelden, 2010), p. 68.

3. Henry David Thoreau, *The Portable Thoreau* (New York: Penguin, 2012), p. 200.

4. Brigid Schulte, *Overwhelmed: Work, Love, and Play When No One Has the Time* (New York: Farrar, Straus & Giroux, 2014), p. 14, Kindle edition.

5. One cost of pouring ourselves into developing social-media personas is a lack of self-knowledge. See D. C. McAllister, "The Loneliness of Not Knowing Ourselves," *The Federalist,* 22 May 2014, accessed 7 June 2014 at http://thefederalist.com/2014/05/22/the-loneliness-of-not-knowing-ourselves.

6. Sendhil Mullainathan and Eldar Shafir, *Scarcity: Why Having Too Little Means So Much* (New York: Times Books, 2013).

7. See books like Uri Gneezy and John A. List, *The Why Axis: Hidden Motives and the Undiscovered Economics of Everyday Life* (New York: PublicAffairs, 2013); Erik Larson, *The Naked Consumer: How Our Private Lives Become Public Commodities* (New York: Henry Holt, 1992); and Richard Ott, *Creating Demand* (Burr Ridge, Ill.: Irwin Professional Publishing, 1992).

8. This phrase is quoted in William Cavanaugh's important short work called *Being Consumed: Economics and Christian Desire* (Grand Rapids: Eerdmans, 2008).

9. For more on desire and consumption, see Cavanaugh's *Being Consumed*.

10. John Helliwell, Richard Layard, and Jeffrey Sachs, "The World Happiness Report," accessed 7 June 2014 at http://www.earth.columbia.edu/sitefiles/file/Sachs%20Writing/2012/World%20Happiness%20Report.pdf.

11. Thomas Merton, *The Inner Experience: Notes on Contemplation* (New York: HarperCollins, 2013).

12. Schulte, *Overwhelmed*, p. 26, Kindle edition.

13. Schulte, *Overwhelmed*, p. 27, Kindle edition.

14. Schulte, *Overwhelmed*, p. 27, Kindle edition.

15. Harmut Rosa, "Social Acceleration: Ethical and Political Consequences of a Desynchronized High-Speed Society," *Constellations* 10 (2003): 8.

16. Chuck DeGroat, *Leaving Egypt: Finding God in the Wilderness Places* (Grand Rapids: Square Inch, 2011).

17. Nicolas Berdyaev, *Slavery and Freedom,* trans. R. M. French (San Rafael, Calif.: Semantron Press, 2009), p. 247.

18. Again, Cavanaugh addresses this elusive freedom well in *Being Consumed,* asking whether or not the free market is, in fact, free. He casts his vision of freedom in the Christian story, with an eye toward the ultimate aim of human life.

19. John Robinson, *Time for Life: The Surprising Ways Americans Use Their Time* (University Park: Pennsylvania State University, 1997).

20. Schulte, *Overwhelmed*, p. 4, Kindle edition.

21. See Klout.com.

Notes to Chapter 2

1. The talk can be found here: https://www.ted.com/talks/brene_brown_on_vulnerability.

2. Brené Brown, *The Gifts of Imperfection: Let Go of Who You Think You're Supposed to Be and Embrace Who You Are* (BookMobile: Kindle Edition), Kindle locations 1027-1029.

3. Brown, *The Gifts of Imperfection,* Kindle locations 1039-1042.

4. See Daniel Siegel, *The Developing Mind: How Relationships and the Brain Interact to Shape Who We Are,* 2nd ed. (New York: Guilford Press, 2012).

5. This doesn't minimize or exclude the reality of an arrogant striving for perfection, but simply places it in a larger narrative.

6. Karen Horney, *New Ways in Psychoanalysis* (New York: Horton & Co., 1939), p. 239.

7. Horney, *New Ways in Psychoanalysis,* p. 243.

8. Names, characteristics, and minor details have been changed to protect confidentiality.

9. An early, comprehensive work is John Rowan, *Subpersonalities: The People Inside of Us* (New York: Routledge, 1990).

10. The "deeper voice" is something I'll address later, but I believe it's my "life, hidden in Christ" (Col. 3:3).

11. Richard Schwartz, *Internal Family Systems Therapy* (New York: Guilford Press, 1995).

12. In saying this, I don't intend to de-mythologize faith. The psychological and the spiritual often name the same realities with different words. However, I am wary of hyper-spiritualizing.

13. Kristin Neff, *Self-Compassion* (New York: HarperCollins, 2011).

14. Neff contends that this movement has led to a culture of narcissism, which has been explored in a variety of recent works on the millennial generation.

15. Neff, *Self-Compassion,* p. 191.

16. Fay Vincent, quoted in Ernest Kurtz and Katherine Ketcham, *The Spirituality of Imperfection: Storytelling and the Journey to Wholeness* (New York: Bantam, 1992), p. 1.

17. Elsie Landström, "Song to My Other Self," in *Inward Light,* No. 67, quoted in Elizabeth O'Connor, *Our Many Selves* (New York: Harper & Row, 1971), p. 35.

Notes to Chapter 3

1. I tell this story in detail in my previous book, *Toughest People to Love* (Grand Rapids: Eerdmans, 2014), Ch. 6.

2. Rom. 7:15, NIV.

3. I'm indebted to the classic work and research of Daniel J. Siegel, *The Developing Mind,* 2nd ed. (New York: Guilford Press, 2012).

4. Richard Schwartz, *Internal Family Systems Therapy* (New York: Guilford Press, 1995).

5. Daniel J. Siegel, *The Mindful Brain* (New York: W. W. Norton, 2007), p. 4.

6. Iain McGilchrist, *The Master and His Emissary* (New Haven: Yale University Press, 2010), Kindle locations 210-212.

7. McGilchrist, *The Master and His Emissary,* Kindle location 2275.

8. Royal Society for the Encouragement of the Arts, "The Divided Brain and the Making of the Western World," YouTube, accessed 20 July 2014 at http://youtu.be/SbUHxC4wiWk.

9. McGilchrist, *The Master and His Emissary,* Kindle location 286.

10. McGilchrist, *The Master and His Emissary,* Kindle location 356.

11. Daniel J. Siegel, *Mindsight: The New Science of Personal Transformation* (New York: Random House, 2009), Kindle locations 100-104.

12. Richard Rohr, *Falling Upward: A Spirituality for the Two Halves of Life* (San Francisco: Jossey-Bass, 2011), p. 151.

13. Curt Thompson, *The Anatomy of the Soul* (Carol Stream, Ill.: Tyndale, 2010), p. 38.

14. Thompson, *The Anatomy of the Soul,* p. 39.

Notes to Chapter 4

1. Mary Oliver, "The Journey," in *Dream Work* by Mary Oliver (New York: Atlantic Monthly Press, 1986), p. 38.

2. Pablo Neruda, "We Are Many": access at http://www.poemhunter.com/poem/we-are-many/.

3. Thomas Kelly, *A Testament of Devotion* (New York: HarperCollins, 1992), p. 9.

4. Kelly, *A Testament of Devotion,* p. 6.

5. Søren Kierkegaard, *Papers and Journals* (London: Penguin, 1996), p. 295.

6. See http://www.poetryfoundation.org/poem/173654.

7. Derek Walcott, "Love after Love," in *The Poetry of Derek Walcott, 1984-2013* (New York: Farrar, Straus & Giroux, 1987), p. 227.

8. Fleur Adcock, "Weathering," in *Poems 1960-2000* by Fleur Adcock (Northumberland, Eng.: Bloodaxe Books, 2010).

9. This is the (slightly altered) slogan of Christian Mingle, a popular online dating site.

Notes to Chapter 5

1. Dale Allison Jr., "Matthew's First Two Words," in *Studies in Matthew* (Grand Rapids: Baker Academic, 2005), pp. 157-62.

2. I've written about the significance of the Exodus story as a way to "re-story" our lives today in *Leaving Egypt: Finding God in the Wilderness Places* (Grand Rapids: Square Inch, 2011).

3. Parker Palmer, *A Hidden Wholeness* (San Francisco: Jossey-Bass, 2004), p. 5.

4. Simon Tugwell, *The Beatitudes: Soundings in Christian Traditions* (Springfield, Ill.: Templegate, 1980), p. 28.

5. Tugwell, *The Beatitudes,* p. 130.

6. Recognizing that both skeptics and followers of Jesus might be reading this chapter, I want to point out that I'm not trying to defend the historicity of the first chapters of Genesis. This is a story, however, that anchors the entire biblical narrative for Christians.

7. Dietrich Bonhoeffer, *Dietrich Bonhoeffer Works, Vol. 8: Letters and Papers from Prison,* trans. Eberhard Bethge (Minneapolis: Augsburg Fortress, 2009), p. 304.

8. A. W. Tozer, *Preparing for Jesus' Return: Daily Live the Blessed Hope,* ed. James L. Snyder (Ventura, Calif.: Gospel Light, 2012), p. 28.

Notes to Chapter 6

1. St. Augustine, *Confessions* 3.6.11.

2. You can access the quote here: http://www.netowne.com/angels-christian/mysticism/catherine.htm.

3. C. S. Lewis, *Letters to Malcolm* (New York: Harvest, 1992), p. 69.

4. See Robert Bly, *A Little Book on the Human Shadow* (New York: HarperCollins, 1988).

5. James Finley, *Merton's Palace of Nowhere* (Notre Dame, Ind.: Ave Maria Press, 1978), p. 30.

6. Dietrich Bonhoeffer, *Dietrich Bonhoeffer Works, Vol. 8: Letters and Papers from Prison,* trans. Eberhard Bethge (Minneapolis: Augsburg Fortress, 2009), pp. 221-22.

7. See Gregory of Nyssa, *Homilies on the Beatitudes,* ed. Hubertus R. Drobner and Alberto Viciano (Leiden: Brill, 2000), p. 70.

8. Frederick Buechner, *Telling Secrets* (New York: HarperCollins, 1991), p. 45.

9. Meister Eckhart, *Treatises and Sermons* (San Francisco: Harper & Row, 1958), p. 219.

10. Saint Augustine, *The Confessions of St. Augustine,* trans. Edward Bouverie Pusey (Kindle edition, 2012), Kindle locations 2515-2517.

11. This quotation can be found here: http://www.ccel.org/a/augustine/confessions/confessions.html.

12. David Whyte, in an excerpt from "Crossing the Unknown Sea," at http://www.gratefulness.org/readings/whyte_dsr.htm.

13. Finley, *Merton's Palace of Nowhere,* p. 37.

14. Finley, *Merton's Palace of Nowhere,* p. 50.

15. St. Augustine's commentary on 1 John can be found here: http://www.newadvent.org/fathers/170207.htm.

Notes to Chapter 7

1. Mary Oliver, "Wild Geese," in *Dream Work* by Mary Oliver (New York: Atlantic Monthly Press, 1986), p. 14.

2. Thomas Kelly, *A Testament of Devotion* (New York: HarperOne, 1993), p. 3.

3. John Calvin, *Institutes of the Christian Religion* (Peabody, Mass.: Hendrickson, 2008), p. 447.

4. I am indebted to the poet David Whyte for his insights into the word "only" in Mary Oliver's poetry.

5. St. John's *Dark Night* is available in a variety of forms online in the public domain. This text is available here: http://www.ecatholic2000.com/stjohn/drknt8.shtml.

6. *The Cloud of Unknowing,* from the *Privy Counsel* PC 1: 7-9 136, available in the public domain.

7. I use the word "synthesis" cautiously. I avoid the word "integration." Because I believe the saints and mystics of old are working with the same "text" of God's created world, I'm more inclined to see this as a process of acknowledging what is already deeply connected, resonant, and whole, making necessary distinctions along the way.

8. St. Augustine, *Confessions* 3.6.11.

9. I'm using my own version of exercises I learned many years ago in a wonderful little book by Anthony DeMello called *Sadhana: A Way to God* (New York: Doubleday, 1978).

Notes to Chapter 8

1. Martin L. Smith, *A Season for the Spirit: Readings for the Days of Lent,* Kindle edition (New York: Seabury Classics, 2004), Kindle Locations 468-473.

2. Daniel Siegel, *Pocket Guide to Interpersonal Neurobiology: An Integrative Handbook of the Mind,* Kindle edition (New York: W. W. Norton, 2012), p. 339.

3. Siegel, *Pocket Guide to Interpersonal Neurobiology,* pp. 134-35.

4. Curt Thompson, *Anatomy of the Soul* (Carol Stream, Ill.: Tyndale, 2010), p. 77.

5. Smith, *A Season for the Spirit,* Kindle Locations 493-495.

6. Although I'm a licensed therapist, I'm not certified as an IFS therapist for a variety of reasons, not the least being that I've been through twenty-five years of education, including doctoral work. Let's just say that while a "part" of me thought I ought to get this certification, my Self was able to relax and say, "I think you've done enough, Chuck. Trust what you've learned." Thus, my own musings on IFS are just that — my own.

7. Within my own Christian narrative, I understand the True Self to be my deepest self in God, while in IFS the Self is inherently ennobled. While there isn't sufficient space here to make a significant anthropological critique of IFS, I do my best in this book to reframe some of the core concepts. See Chapter 6, especially, for more on this True Self.

8. Although IFS is a secular model, I find these eight characteristics remarkably akin to the nine biblical fruits of the Spirit: love, joy, peace, forbearance, kindness, goodness, faithfulness, gentleness, and self-control.

9. I'm not altogether settled on the language of "parts," though I can honestly say, "A part of me likes it." Some psychologists use the language of ego-states, subpersonalities, mind-states, or voices. But parts language is more accessible to laypeople.

10. While IFS provides a model for acting with compassion toward potentially an-

gry and reactive parts of ourselves, it in no way condones abuse. Confronting abusive behavior is absolutely necessary, though the long-term work of healing will require self-compassionate inner work.

Notes to Chapter 9

1. I don't want to suggest that leaving a church or even a marriage is a "bad" thing. What I'm diagnosing here is a more "global" phenomenon. To be sure, churches and relationships that are abusive and destructive ought to be confronted and perhaps even run from.

2. C. S. Lewis, *Mere Christianity* (New York: Touchstone, 1996), p. 190.

3. I highly recommend Daniel Wolpert, *Creating a Life with God* (Nashville: Upper Room, 2003). Wolpert introduces a variety of helpful practices used by Christians throughout the century.

4. St. Teresa of Ávila, *Interior Castle,* trans. Mirabai Starr (New York: Riverhead, 2003).

5. See Thomas Keating on the method of centering prayer: http: www.cpt.org/ files/WS%20-%20Centering%20Prayer.pdf.

6. I recommend the following works: Martin Laird, *Into the Silent Land* (New York: Oxford University Press, 2006); Thomas Merton, *Contemplative Prayer* (London: Dartman, Longman & Todd, 2006); and James Finley, *The Contemplative Heart* (Notre Dame: Sorin, 2000). For the theological perspectives on this prayer of union, see *Partakers of the Divine Nature: The History and Development of Deification in the Christian Traditions,* ed. Michael J. Christensen and Jeffrey A. Wittung (Grand Rapids: Baker Academic, 2007); J. Todd Billings, *Union with Christ* (Grand Rapids: Baker Academic, 2011); Douglas Fairbairn, *Life in the Trinity* (Downers Grove, Ill.: IVP Press, 2009); and Hans Urs von Balthasar, *Prayer* (Einsiedeln, Switzerland: Johannes Verlag, 1955).

7. St. Augustine, *The Works of St. Augustine,* trans. Edmund Hill (New York: New City Press, 2009).

8. Augustine, *Confessions* 3.6.11.

9. For more on this, see James K. A. Smith, *Desiring the Kingdom* (Grand Rapids: Baker Academic, 2009), and Robert Webber, *Ancient-Future Faith* (Grand Rapids: Baker Academic, 1999).

10. See http://www.earlychristianwritings.com/text/diognetus-roberts.html.

11. Quoted in W. Lucas Collins, *Thucydides* (New York: John Alden, 1883), p. 154.

12. Quoted in J. C. Ayer, *A Sourcebook for Ancient Church History* (New York: Charles Scribner, 1922), p. 21.

13. Thomas Merton, *The Inner Experience: Notes on Contemplation* (San Francisco: HarperSanFrancisco, 2004), p. 18.

14. See http://www.poetryfoundation.org/poem/173654.